H. RH. 2656.

Mel Bay's

Rock Harmonica

Power Licks, High-End Licks & Speed

Learn two of Rock's all-time great harm
"Whammer Jammer" and **"Room to M**
written by Jason Ricci "How to Be a Great

School of the Blues Lesson Series

by David Barrett

CD1 Contents

1 Welcome
2 Ex. 2.1 Bending for Expression
3 Ex. 2.2 Bending and Going to an Unbent Note
4 Ex. 2.3 Half Step Control on Holes 2 and 3
5 Ex. 2.4 Starting in the Bent Position 1
6 Ex. 2.5 Starting in the Bent Position 2
7 Ex. 3.1 Major Pent Scale
8 Ex. 3.2 Major Pent Scale Half Notes
9 Ex. 3.3 Major Pent Scale Quarter Notes
10 Ex. 3.4 Major Pent Scale Swing Eighths
11 Ex. 3.5 Major Pent Scale Triplets
12 Ex. 3.6 Major Pent Scale Eighth Notes
13 Ex. 3.7 Major Pent Scale Sixteenths Notes
14 Ex. 3.8 Major Pent Scale Holes 1 to 3
15 Ex. 3.9 Major Pent Scale Holes 1 to 4
16 Ex. 3.10 Major Pent Scale Holes 3 to 6
17 Ex. 3.11 Major Pent Scale Holes 6 to 10
18 Ex. 3.12 Major Pent Scale Entire Range
19 Ex. 3.13 Major Pent Scale Backing Track
20 Ex. 3.15 Major Pent Scale 12 Bar Blues
21 Ex. 3.16 Major Pent Scale 12 Bar Blues Play-Along
22 Ex. 3.17 Blues Scale
23 Ex. 3.18 Blues Scale Half Notes
24 Ex. 3.19 Blues Scale Quarter Notes
25 Ex. 3.20 Blues Scale Swing Eighths
26 Ex. 3.21 Blues Scale Triplets
27 Ex. 3.22 Blues Scale Eighth Notes
28 Ex. 3.23 Blues Scale Sixteenths Notes
29 Ex. 3.24 Blues Scale Holes 1 to 3
30 Ex. 3.25 Blues Scale Holes 1 to 4
31 Ex. 3.26 Blues Scale Holes 3 to 6
32 Ex. 3.27 Blues Scale Holes 6 to 10
33 Ex. 3.28 Blues Scale Entire Range
34 Ex. 3.29 Blues Scale Play-Along Track
35 Ex. 3.31 Blues Scale 12 Bar Blues
36 Ex. 3.32 Blues Scale 12 Bar Blues Play-Along Track
37 Ex. 4.1 C Major Scale
38 Ex. 4.2 to 4.4 Octave Sub
39 Ex. 4.5 Breathing and Movement Patterns
40 Ex. 4.6 to 4.7 Backtracking
41 Ex. 4.8 to 4.13 Examples
42 Ex. 4.14 to 4.18 Examples
43 Ex. 4.19 to 4.21 Examples
44 Ex. 4.22 to 4.26 Examples
45 Ex. 5.1 to 5.4 Power Licks
46 Ex. 5.5 to 5.8 Power Licks
47 Ex. 5.9 to 5.13 Power Licks
48 Ex. 5.14 to 5.20 Power Licks
49 Ex. 6.1 to 6.3 Scales
50 Ex. 6.4 to 6.7 Chords
51 Ex. 6.10 to 6.12 Chord Qualities
52 Ex. 6.14 12 Bar Blues Arpeggios
53 Ex. 6.15 to 6.18 12 Chord Scales
54 Ex. 7.1 12 Bar Blues
55 Ex. 7.2 12 Bar Blues with Quick Change
56 Ex. 7.3 16 Bar Blues
57 Ex. 7.4 2 Bar Ex 1
58 Ex. 7.5 2 Bar Ex 2
59 Ex. 7.6 2 Bar Ex 3
60 Ex. 7.7 2 Bar Ex 4

CD2 Contents

1 Ex. 7.8 2 Bar Ex 5
2 Ex. 7.9 2 Bar Ex 6
3 Ex. 7.10 4 Bar Ex 1
4 Ex. 7.11 4 Bar Ex 2
5 Ex. 7.12 to 7.13 Voice Leading
6 Ex. 7.14 8 Bar
7 Ex. 7.15 12 Bar Altered
8 Ex. 7.16 12 Bar Long V
9 Ex. 8.1 Head
10 Ex. 8.3 Hook
11 Ex. 8.5 to 8.7 Sequences
12 Ex. 8.8 Room to Move
13 Ex. 8.8 Room to Move Play-Along Track
14 Whammer Jammer Opening
15 Whammer Jammer Chorus 1
16 Whammer Jammer Chorus 2
17 Whammer Jammer Chorus 3
18 Whammer Jammer Chorus 4
19 Whammer Jammer Chorus 5
20 Whammer Jammer Chorus 6
21 Whammer Jammer Chorus 7
22 Whammer Jammer Chorus 8
23 Whammer Jammer Chorus 9
24 Whammer Jammer Chorus 10
25 Whammer Jammer
26 Whammer Jammer [20per Slow]
27 Whammer Jammer Play-Along Track
28 Butter Strut
29 Butter Strut [20per Slow]
30 Butter Strut Play-Along Track
31 Butter Strut Play-Along Track no Guitar

MEL BAY

1 2 3 4 5 6 7 8 9 0

© 2011 BY MEL BAY PUBLICATIONS, INC., PACIFIC, MO 63069.
ALL RIGHTS RESERVED. INTERNATIONAL COPYRIGHT SECURED. B.M.I. MADE AND PRINTED IN U.S.A.
No part of this publication may be reproduced in whole or in part, or stored in a retrieval system, or transmitted in any form or by any means, electronic, mechanical, photocopy, recording, or otherwise, without written permission of the publisher.

Visit us on the Web at www.melbay.com — E-mail us at email@melbay.com

Table of Contents

What is Rock Harmonica?

The blanket term "Rock" is used to describe a musical genre that covers over six decades of musical diversity. From its early Rock and Roll roots to a host of subgenres, including Folk Rock, Blues-Rock, Jazz-Rock Fusion, Soft Rock, Heavy Metal, Hard Rock, Progressive Rock, Punk Rock, Grunge and Indie Rock to name but a few. The question for this book is, "What does Rock mean to harmonica players?"

- A style heavily influenced by Blues (think blues on steroids)
- Heavy use of bluesy/dark notes (blues scale)
- Hook-driven (main lick that drives a song)
- Fast (tends to more wow-factor and less subtlety)
- Thick textures (two-hole combinations for example)
- Twelve bar blues progressions; progressions that use the same chords as the twelve bar blues (**I**, **IV** and **V** chords); and progressions that utilize other chords in addition to those of the standard twelve bar blues.

Our most prominent Rock players are well-studied Blues harmonica players: John Mayall (Bluesbreakers), Paul Butterfield, Magic Dick (J Geils Band), Kim Wilson (Fabulous Thunderbirds), Huey Lewis (Huey Lewis and the News), Norton Buffalo (Steve Miller Band), and most recently Jason Ricci (New Blood). As a player, Jason Ricci epitomizes what's needed to be a great Rock harmonica player in today's music scene. His strong roots in blues harmonica and strong grounding in music theory enable him to deal with the challenges that Rock music presents... and that brings us to what this book is all about...

What this Book Has To Offer YOU!

You're a harmonica player with some blues roots... in fact you love blues, but deep down inside you yearn to Rock! You, and your buds, think you can blow pretty well. That's where we start. You can move around the harmonica well. You know how to bend—maybe not with a lot of control, but you can do it. Possibly you've dabbled with tongue blocking—but not seriously. You're extremely turned off by studying music theory, but you know you'll need some of it to be able to keep up with the other musicians, and you hate the feeling of not knowing what's going on or how to deal with blues songs not using standard blues progressions.

In this book you'll learn:

- How to control your bends better (half step control)
- Speed licks
- High-end licks
- How to play super bluesy (notes and textures)
- How to play and construct hooks (the main element of Rock songwriting and accompaniment playing)
- How to deal with and play over the common chord progressions used in Rock
- Music theory and how it relates to playing Rock harmonica.

You'll learn how to play the most famous Rock harmonica instrumental of all time, Magic Dick's "Whammer Jammer!" And on top of this, I've written an original Rock harmonica instrumental for you ("Butter Strut"), that's much heavier in feel and more progressive in nature—to contrast with the more classic "Whammer Jammer."

What You'll Need

C and A Major diatonic harmonicas (this is the standard ten-hole harmonica), a CD player, and the time to dig in and learn!

Chapter 1 - **A Word about Notation and Embouchure**

The harmonica notation in this book is based on the ten-hole diatonic harmonica played in second position. Harmonica players use a wide variety of harmonica keys in their music. For ease of reading, all harmonica parts played on the ten-hole diatonic harmonica will use the key signature of C major. This will place you in the pitch set of a C major harmonica. Through years of teaching, writing and conducting seminars, I have found this method of notation to be the fastest for translating musical thought. Diagrammed below is a C major ten-hole diatonic harmonica.

BLOW ⟶	C	E	G	C	E	G	C	E	G	C
C	1	2	3	4	5	6	7	8	9	10
DRAW ⟶	D	G	B	D	F	A	B	D	F	A

Harmonica Tablature

You'll notice in the diagram that each hole has a corresponding number. In the tablature, the number corresponding to the hole will be under the notational symbol for the note to be played. When a note stands by itself, the note is to be drawn (inhaled). When a number is followed with a plus (+), the note is to be blown (exhaled). If the note is to be bent, a series of slashes will be notated to the right of the number. Each slash represents a half-step bend. For example: three draw (3) is "B", and bent down a half step it's "B-flat" and is notated as 3'. Three draw bent down a whole step is "A" and is notated as 3". Three draw bent down a whole step and one half (minor third bend) is "A-flat" and is notated as 3'''. Diagrammed below is the entire bend chart for the C major diatonic harmonica.

Whole Step Bend (") ⟶										B♭
½ Step Bend (') ⟶								E♭	G♭	B
BLOW ⟶	C	E	G	C	E	G	C	E	G	C
C	1	2	3	4	5	6	7	8	9	10
DRAW ⟶	D	G	B	D	F	A	B	D	F	A
½ Step Bend (') ⟶	D♭	G♭	B♭	D♭		A♭				
Whole Step Bend (") ⟶		F	A							
1-½ Step Bend (''') ⟶			A♭							

These basics will get you going in my notation system. A notation key is provided for you at the back of this book if you see a symbol that you're not familiar with.

Embouchure

Embouchure is a term we use for how we place our lips on the harmonica—more specifically, the placement of our lips, tongue and mouth cavity. Anyone who's familiar with my work knows that I'm a big fan of tongue blocking to create a single note. The truth is that Rock has not traditionally relied a lot on tongue blocking skills. So, in this book, however you create a single note is up to you… you're not a beginning player, so I don't need to lecture you on how to move around the harmonica. With that said, the harmonica's greatest asset is in its ability to present notes in so many different ways, many of which can only be done in a tongue block. If you're not familiar with tongue blocking, I recommend you explore some of the methods that I list at the end of this book and start your journey.

Chapter 2 - **Bending**

In the harmonica world there are two main techniques that we spend a lifetime studying: bending and tongue blocking. Since Rock harmonica focuses less on tongue blocking (though "Whammer Jammer" has tons of it), your bending skills take front seat. Your ability to play really bluesy, to play really fast, and to play non-twelve bar blues chord changes are all directly related to your bending skills.

Most likely you're already bending on the harmonica, but most players have no idea what creates a bend and how far they can bend on each hole of the harmonica. So, let's dig into a much deeper understanding. We'll do plenty of licks with great bend combinations later in the book.

Bending is achieved by tuning your mouth to the pitch you desire to achieve. Lowering the pitch of your mouth is achieved by two movements of your tongue: 1) your tongue must hump up to slightly constrict the air passage; and 2) it must move back to lower the resonant pitch of your mouth and thus lower the pitch of the reed you intend to bend.

Start by saying the vowel "E" in a draw anywhere on the lower six holes of the harmonica. "E" places the middle/back of your tongue under your upper set of teeth. This sets up the passage where the air will travel. You can feel the air only traveling between the roof of your mouth, the inner-sides of your teeth, and the top of your tongue. The center of the tongue then pushes up (like the "K" in "Key") to squeeze the air stream for the constriction needed (of which not a lot is needed). Then it pulls back to bring the pitch of that reed down. Depending where you hump your tongue, you might have very little movement back for the bend (such as on a 6 draw), or you might need a large amount of movement to create the bend (such as on the 3, 2 and 1 draws).

Each reed is a different length and sounds a different pitch. The longer the reed, the lower the pitch and the slower its vibration. The shorter the reed, the higher its pitch and the faster its vibration. In the bending process, as you move your tongue back for the bend, it's "frequency-pulling" the reed. In other words, as your tongue moves back, the resonant pitch of your mouth lowers and so does the pitch of the reed you're playing. This is best felt by whistling. Whistle a high note, and then slowly slide the pitch down to the lowest note you can achieve. Notice that the wings of your tongue are touching your upper set of teeth; to lower the pitch you move your tongue back, and to raise the pitch your tongue moves forward. The process is the same for bending a note on the harmonica.

For the 6 draw, the front-middle of your tongue will move up and a little back. For the 4 draw, you'll move further up and back. You'll probably find the 4 draw to be one of the easier notes to bend. Reference the diagram at right to get a visual idea of where the tongue will be in relation to the roof of the mouth.

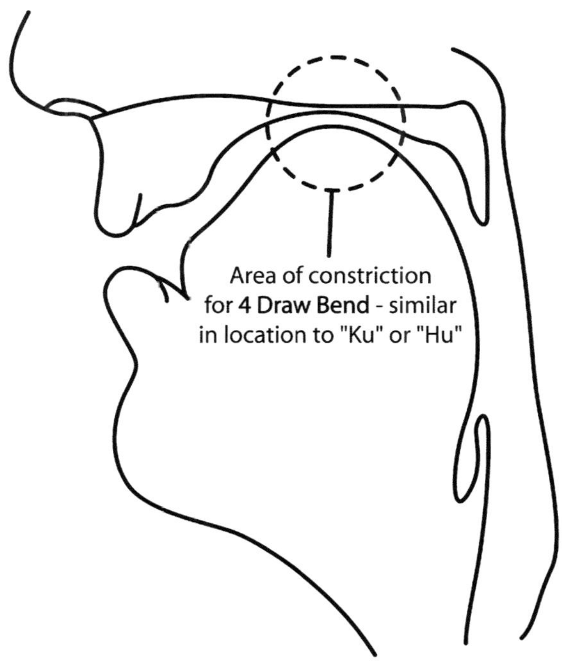

When trying the 3 or 2 draw bend, most players don't move their tongues high enough and far enough back in the mouth. The 3 draw bend is achieved by having your tongue humped up somewhere near your back molars, resting on the gums. For the 2 draw it's further back, most of the time not touching the teeth at all, just the gums; and for the 1 draw it's back and down still further.

When performing the lower bends, you might find it useful to drop your jaw. This lowers the resonant pitch of your mouth and should make it easier to tune your mouth to the bend you wish to play.

Another helpful hint for the lower draw bends is to think of raising the root (also known as the base) of your tongue for the deeper bends. The lowered pitch is achieved by humping up in different places along the length of the tongue. It will be hard to move the middle of the tongue far back enough to achieve the pitch needed for the lower bends. By humping the stem of the tongue up, you're able to access a part of the tongue that's already located very far back in the mouth.

The main point is to experiment! Read this information over and over—you won't get it the first read through. Get to know what your tongue is doing and where it's located relative to other structures in your mouth.

What Notes Can Be Bent

Not every hole (note) on the harmonica can be bent, and not every hole that you can bend produces the same degree of bend. The amount of bend you can achieve on a hole is dictated by the distance (scale interval) between its draw and blow reed. The chromatic scale, which lists every note available in our diatonic music system, is diagrammed below.

A B♭ B C D♭ D E♭ E F G♭ G A♭ A

Let's look at the 1 draw and the 1 blow on the C harmonica. The 1 draw is the note D and the 1 blow is the note C. When playing a 1 draw bend, you can bend down to whatever note is between these two notes. Looking at the chromatic scale above, that gives you the note D-flat. When playing a 2 draw bend, you can bend down to whatever is between the G of the 2 draw and E of the 2 blow. This gives you two notes: G-flat and F. Follow this process up to the 6 draw.

At the seventh hole the harmonica does a back flip of sorts. On holes 1 through 6, the draw notes are higher than the blow notes (1 draw D is higher in the scale than 1 blow C, for example). On the seventh through tenth holes the blows are now higher than the draws. This means that you'll bend the blow notes now. The same bending rule applies for the blow notes… whatever pitches are between the blow and draw reed are what you can play by bending.

Diagrammed below are all the bends available on the C harmonica. Each slash (') represents a half step bend (3 = 3 draw, 3' = 3 draw half step bend, 3" = 3 draw whole step bend and 3"' = 3 draw minor third bend).

Whole Step Bend (") →										B♭
½ Step Bend (') →								E♭	G♭	B
BLOW →	C	E	G	C	E	G	C	E	G	C
C	1	2	3	4	5	6	7	8	9	10
DRAW →	D	G	B	D	F	A	B	D	F	A
½ Step Bend (') →	D♭	G♭	B♭	D♭		A♭				
Whole Step Bend (") →		F	A							
1-½ Step Bend ("') →			A♭							

Bending Exercises

Your first goal is to check that you can bend as far as the harmonica will allow on each of the holes in Example 2.1. Most students find the 6, 5 and 4 draw the easiest holes to bend. Take note that the 5 draw will not give you a full degree of a bend; it will bend down what is called a ***Quartertone***. In other words, you'll only hear a slight bend on the 5 draw, and that is correct. If you find the 3 and 2 draw difficult to bend very far, focus on dropping your jaw slightly and humping the root of the tongue up more to access the back of your mouth better.

Ex. 2.1 – Bending for Expression (Track 2, C Harmonica)

Most players find that their 3 draw jumps in pitch—from a slight bend to a full bend, with nothing in the middle. To remedy this, make sure that your tongue is following the curvature of the roof of your mouth. Chances are that you're moving the tongue back just fine, but the tongue isn't moving up high enough as it moves back. A good visualization is to think like you have a marble sitting on top of your tongue. As you move your tongue back to bend, you must keep it raised up to the roof of your mouth so that the marble doesn't fall down. This consistent distance to the roof of the mouth is what keeps the bend moving down in pitch smoothly until you achieve the deepest tone. Resist the urge to tighten your mouth and ball up the tongue. Keep reminding yourself that you're simply tuning your mouth to the desired pitch to create a bend… no excessive force is needed for this.

The exercise below will help you to bend a note down and move to another note. Pay attention that your bend doesn't release slightly before going to the next note. Also pay attention that your next note isn't played flat because you haven't moved your tongue out of the bend embouchure quickly enough.

Ex. 2.2 – Bending and Going to an Unbent Draw Note (Track 3)

Let's now work to achieve each of the half step bends available on holes 2 and 3. Your ability to control these bends, especially the 3 draw, is crucial in becoming a more advanced player.

Ex. 2.3 – Half Step Control on Holes 2 and 3 (Track 4)

Once you can achieve a clean slide ascending and descending in pitch try to start in the bent position.

Ex. 2.4 – Starting in the Bent Position (Track 5)

Ex. 2.5 – Starting in the Bent Position (Track 6)

Chapter 3 – Scales for Improvising

Even though we'll speak in more detail about these scales later on in the theory section, they also require strong bending control, so it makes sense to dig into these now. It boils down to two scales that you need to be familiar with to play almost any style of music, the ***Blues Scale*** and the ***Major Pentatonic Scale***.

Major Pentatonic Scale

To solo with a light, more major feel, a five note scale called the Major Pentatonic scale is often used. This scale comes from the major scale, with the fourth and seventh scale degrees omitted—giving it a floating quality (this is where the half steps are in the scale—omission of half steps take all of the leading tones away). If the song is in the key of G, then you will use a G major pentatonic scale.

Ex. 3.1 – Major Pentatonic Scale (Track 7)

1	2+	2	3"	3	4	5+	6+	6	7	8	8+	9+	10
D	E	G	A	B	D	E	G	A	B	D	E	G	A
5th	6th	Root	2nd	3rd	5th	6th	Root	2nd	3rd	5th	6th	Root	2nd

Let's now practice this scale in some common rhythms.

Ex. 3.2 – Major Pentatonic Scale: Half Notes (Track 8)

Ex. 3.3 – Major Pentatonic Scale: Quarter Notes (Track 9)

Ex. 3.4 – Major Pentatonic Scale: Swing Eighths (Track 10)

Ex. 3.5 – Major Pentatonic Scale: Triplets (Track 11)

Since you'll play both swing eighths (think shuffle rhythm, like in the examples above) and straight eighths in Rock, we need to practice them both ways. Below are straight eighths and sixteenth notes.

Ex. 3.6 – Major Pentatonic Scale: Eighths (Track 12)

Ex. 3.7 – Major Pentatonic Scale: Sixteenths (Track 13)

Now that you've developed the skill to play this scale in the most common rhythms, it's time to improvise with it. For the following tracks I'll improvise using the limited range notated in our examples below. It's important to get to know each section of the harmonica individually before you try to use its entire range. For each track I'll improvise for a bit and then leave room for you to give it a try.

Do your best to only use the notes of the scale. Let your lick vocabulary drive you, but stay alert so that you can change a note you would normally play outside of the scale to a note that's in the scale. You're basically watching yourself in the third person and saying to yourself, "Watch out, you normally go to a 2" in this run, but you have to change it to 2+." It's this constant assessment that you make as you play that will make this successful. We'll use the rock beat for these examples.

Ex. 3.8 – Major Pentatonic Scale: Holes 1 through 3 (Track 14)

Ex. 3.9 – Major Pentatonic Scale: Holes 1 through 4 (Track 15)

Ex. 3.10 – Major Pentatonic Scale: Holes 3 through 6 (Track 16)

Ex. 3.11 – Major Pentatonic Scale: Holes 6 though 10 (Track 17)

Ex. 3.12 – Major Pentatonic Scale: Entire Range (Track 18)

Ex. 3.13 – Play-Along Track Only (Track 19)

Our previous examples played to a backing track that stayed on the **I** Chord. Though this scale can be used over any chord in the blues progression, there are of course notes that if held can be overly dissonant. Detailed below is the same scale as in Example 3.1 but with the addition of chords below each note. If you see **IV** under a note, that note will sound good when held on that chord. The same for the **V** Chord. Your goal is to hit one note of the chord and hold it for just a bit to tip your hat to the chord change, then go off and improvise without worrying about what notes should match that chord. You can of course adhere closer to the notes of the chord change, but a strong presentation of one of these notes does the trick very well.

Ex. 3.14 – Major Pentatonic Scale w/Chords

1	2+	2	3"	3	4	5+	6+	6	7	8	8+	9+	10
V	IV	IV	V		V	IV	IV	V		V	IV	IV	V

Ex. 3.15 – Major Pentatonic Scale: Entire Range w/12 Bar Blues Progression (Track 20)

Ex. 3.16 – 12 Bar Blues Play-Along Track (Track 21)

Blues Scale

To solo with a darker, more minor feel, as in most Blues-based and aggressive Rock, the six-note scale called the ***Blues Scale*** is often used. This scale comes from the minor scale, with the second and sixth scale degrees omitted and a flat-5 added. If a song is in the key of G, then you'll use a G blues scale.

Ex. 3.17 – Blues Scale (Track 22)

1+	1'	1	2"	2	3'	4+	4'	4	5	6+	6'	6	7+	8	9	9+
C	D♭	D	F	G	B♭	C	D♭	D	F	G	A♭	A	C	D	F	G
4th	♭5th	5th	♭7th	Root	♭3rd	4+	♭5th	5th	♭7th	Root	♭2nd	2nd	4th	5th	♭7th	Root

Let's now practice this scale in the common rhythms.

Ex. 3.18 – Blues Scale: Half Notes (Track 23)

Ex. 3.19 – Blues Scale: Quarter Notes (Track 24)

Ex. 3.20 – Blues Scale: Swing Eighths (Track 25)

Ex. 3.21 – Blues Scale: Triplets (Track 26)

Below are straight eighths and sixteenth notes.

Ex. 3.22 – Blues Scale: Eighths (Track 27)

Ex. 3.23 – Blues Scale: Sixteenths (Track 28)

Now that you've developed the skill to play this scale in the most common rhythms, it's again time to improvise with it. Most players make the mistake of playing the 2+ (major 6th) where 2" needs to be used (flat-7th), and forgetting to bend the 3 draw (major 3rd) down to 3' (minor 3rd).

Ex. 3.24 – Blues Scale: Holes 1 through 3 (Track 29)

Ex. 3.25 – Blues Scale: Holes 1 through 4 (Track 30)

Ex. 3.26 – Blues Scale: Holes 3 through 6 (Track 31)

Ex. 3.27 – Blues Scale: Holes 6 though 10 (Track 32)

Ex. 3.28 – Blues Scale: Entire Range (Track 33)

Ex. 3.29 – Play-Along Track (Track 34)

Let's take a look how these notes fare over the twelve bar blues progression.

Ex. 3.30 – Blues Scale w/Chords

Ex. 3.31 – Blues Scale: Entire Range w/12 Bar Blues Progression (Track 35)

Ex. 3.32 – 12 Bar Blues Play-Along Track (Track 36)

Context

Both scales can be played over a major backing, and the blues scale can be played over a minor backing as well. Learn and experiment with each of these scales separately at first to feel what each scale has to offer in both mood and technique. After you have this foundation, merge the two scales together in your major soloing. Viewing this as one scale allows you to move between darker, more bluesy lines with the blues scale and lighter, more major lines with the major pentatonic scale to achieve the feel you desire.

Either scale can be used over all chord changes within a twelve bar blues progression, but keep in mind that some notes of the scale will clash with certain chords. If a note from the scale is a chord tone, it's fine. If a note isn't a chord tone, it will need to be resolved to a chord tone. If the non-chord tone is used in passing in a more active line, then no special treatment is needed.

The soloing scale is based on the key of the song. For example, in G major, the notes of the major pentatonic scale are G, A, B, D, and E. The G is the root of the **I** Chord, fifth of the **IV7** Chord and fourth of the **V7** Chord. The A is the second of the **I** Chord (or ninth if held), sixth of the **IV7** Chord and fifth of the **V7** Chord. The B is the third of the **I** Chord, major seventh of the **IV7** Chord (very dissonant) and sixth (or 13th) of the **V7** Chord. The D is the fifth of the **I** Chord, second of the **IV7** Chord (or 9th) and root of the **V7** Chord. The E is the sixth of the **I** Chord, third of the **IV7** Chord and the second (or 9th) of the **V7** Chord.

Reference Chapter 6 for more of an understanding of these concepts. If this is all very confusing right now, you're not alone—it takes time and effort to absorb this. It's okay to do this intuitively by playing over the changes by ear at first, but keep in mind that your developing ear may not hear if a note matches well or not. Your ultimate goal is to be aware of the relationship of each note you play over a given chord.

Homework

Memorize these two scales. In the accompanying recording I play solos over the chord changes taught. In some cases I use the notes of the chord, but in many I'm just using these scales. If you become familiar with these scales you'll be able to pick up most of what I play relatively easily.

Chapter 4 – **Speed and High-End Licks**

Mastering the High End of the Harmonica

Playing the high end of the harmonica is not hard—you just need to dig in and do it! Blues players don't have a lot of licks to study because blues harp players spend most of their time on the lower six holes for the tone and vast array of textures available. Here are a couple of principles that will help you in your quest to become a great high-end player.

Note Layout

One only has to look as far as the major scale on the harmonic (C major scale on the C major harmonica) to see that the high end contains the same notes as the low end minus the seventh scale degree B (without bending that is). Take a look at and play the three octaves of the same scale below. Also look at the actual pitches you're playing by referencing the C Harmonica Diagram below.

Ex. 4.1 – C Major Scale: Three Octaves (Track 37)

1+	1	2+	2"	2	3"	3	4+	4+	4	5+	5	6+	6	7	7+	7+	8	8+	9	9+	10	10'+	10+
C	D	E	F	G	A	B	C	C	D	E	F	G	A	B	C	C	D	E	F	G	A	B	C

C	1	2	3	4	5	6	7	8	9	10
BLOW →	C	E	G	C	E	G	C	E	G	C
DRAW →	D	G	B	D	F	A	B	D	F	A

Let's make some generalizations: A blow note is always a blow note, in all ranges of the harmonica. If you play C on the 1+, the note C is also available as a blow higher up the range of the harmonica. And a draw note is always a draw note (except for the 2 draw G).

That makes it a bit easier. What gets challenging is that across the range of the harmonica the relative order of notes changes. For an example we'll reference the notes available on the C Harmonica, including standard bending (see chart below). To play F to G on the low end, we play 2" to 2; on the middle of the harmonica we play F on the 5 draw (not a bend) and then move over one hole to the 6 blow to get G; and finally we play 9 draw for F and just blow (no movement) to play G. What a pain!

C	1	2	3	4	5	6	7	8	9	10
Whole Step Bend (") →										B♭
½ Step Bend (') →								E♭	G♭	B
BLOW →	C	E	G	C	E	G	C	E	G	C
DRAW →	D	G	B	D	F	A	B	D	F	A
½ Step Bend (') →	D♭	G♭	B♭	D♭		A♭				
Whole Step Bend (") →		F	A							
1-½ Step Bend (''') →			A♭							

One great way to become comfortable with playing on the high end is to take licks you're already familiar with and move them up an octave. As longs as your licks are not bend-focused (2" and 3" are okay), then this works great. Below are some examples.

Ex. 4.2 (Track 38)

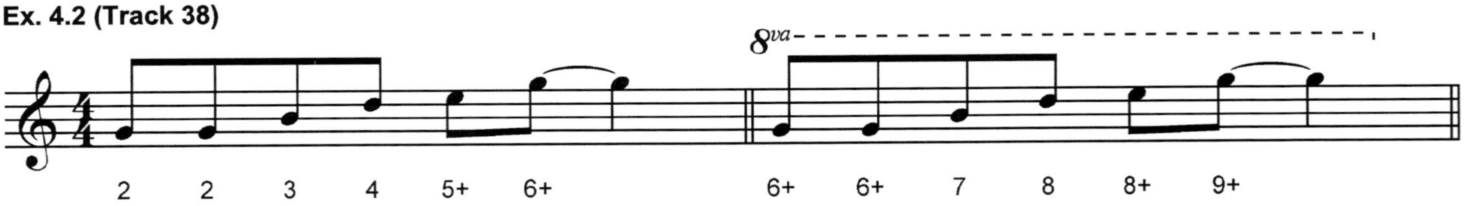

Ex. 4.3

Ex. 4.4

Speed Playing

The keys to being able to play fast runs on the harmonica are: 1) to thoroughly know the scales we have spoken of so far (Major Pentatonic and Blues); 2) to search out both breathing and movement patterns on the harmonica; and 3) to utilize back-tracking to make lines seem longer (well, they are longer—they just use less holes than one may expect).

Breathing and Movement Patterns

To understand this is simple: the idea is to group together as many blow notes or draw notes as you can in a phrase, and give them a repetitive breathing pattern. Our example lick below does this very well. The breathing pattern uses three draws, then three blows, then three draws, etc. The movement pattern is: note, down, back; then change to the next note in the basic scale of the harmonica and repeat with note, down, back, etc. The combining of these two elements creates a phrase that can be played very fast.

Ex. 4.5 (Track 39)

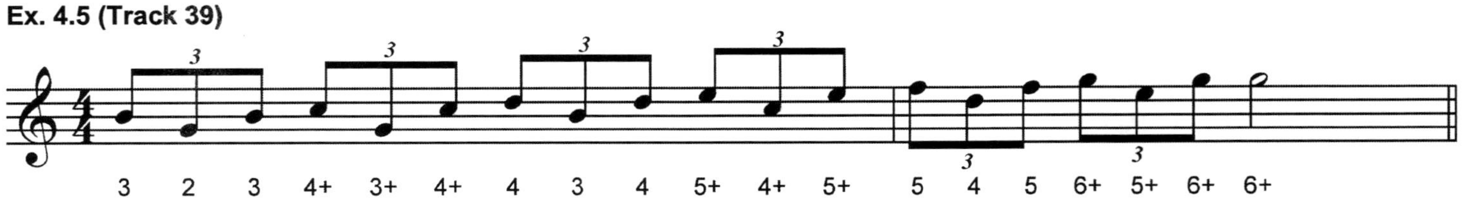

Backtracking

This technique gives the listener the impression that we're playing a lot more notes than we are. Well, to be exact, we are playing a lot of notes, but we're repeating many of them. The idea is pretty simple: play some notes ascending or descending and then backtrack a couple of notes and repeat it. Here are a couple of examples of this.

Ex. 4.6 (Track 40)

Ex. 4.7

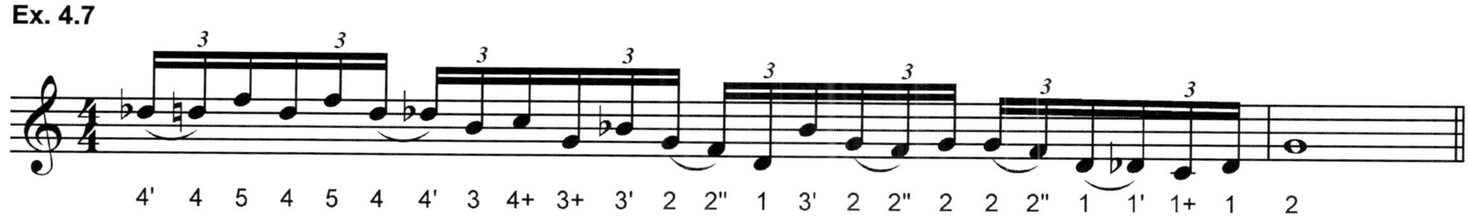

Let's now dig into a whole bunch of cool speed licks. Speed licks tend to have a strong focus on bending, so these licks will take your bending skills to the next level. We'll also focus heavily on high-end playing.

Let's start with some great repetitive patterns, the backbone of speed licks.

Ex. 4.8 (Track 41)

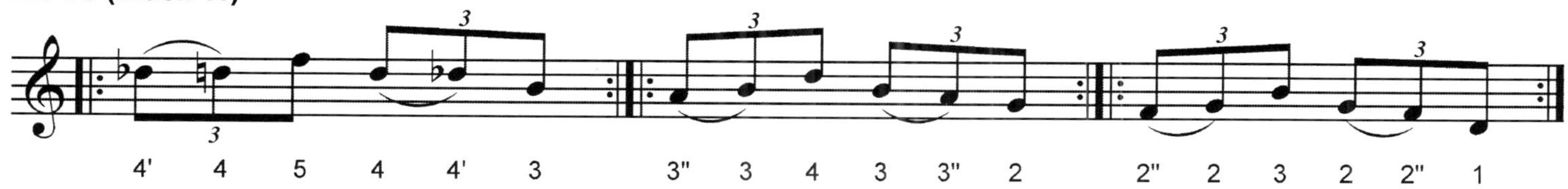

Ex. 4.9

Ex. 4.10

Ex. 4.11

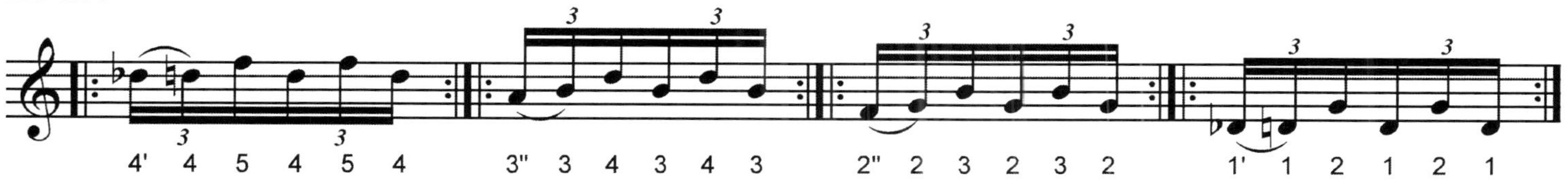

Ex. 4.12

Ex. 4.13

Ex. 4.14 (Track 42)

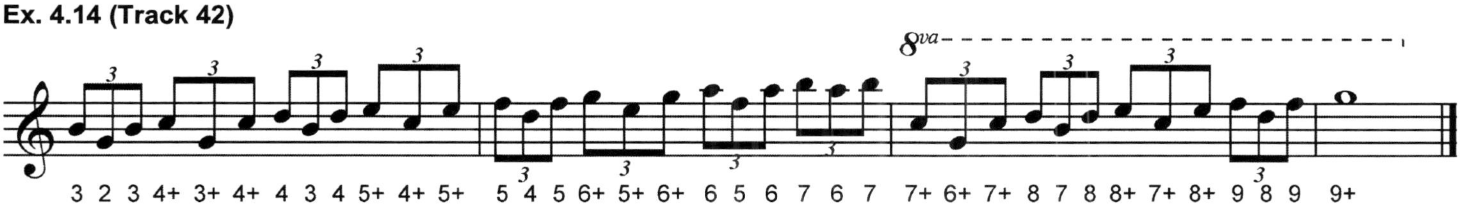

Let's now dig into some more speed licks.

Ex. 4.15

4 5 4' 3 2 (3+)(2+)(1+) 3' 2 2" 1 2

Ex. 4.16

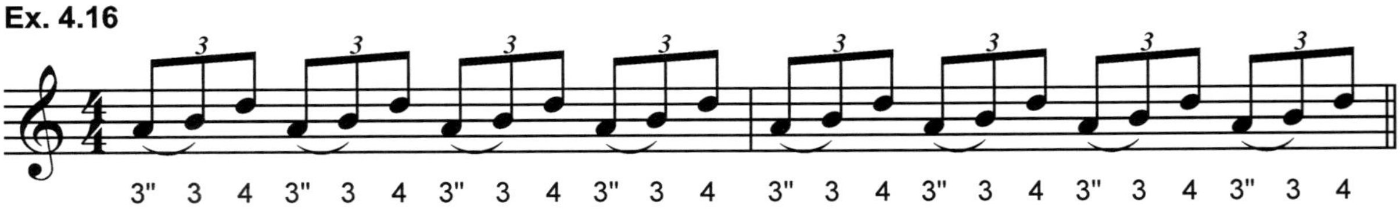

3" 3 4 3" 3 4 3" 3 4 3" 3 4 3" 3 4 3" 3 4 3" 3 4 3" 3 4

Ex. 4.17

2 1 2 1 2" 1 1' 1 2 1 2 1 2" 1 1' 1 2 1 2 1 2" 1 1' 1 4'/3' 4 4' 3 4+ 3 2

Ex. 4.18

4 5 4 4+ 3+ 4+ 3' 2 4 5 4 4+ 3+ 4+ 3' 4+

Ex. 4.19 (Track 43)

Be aware of the unbent 3 draw in our next lick. This will sound fine with a major backing, but anything with a dark feel will make this lick sound awkward.

2" 2 3 2 3 2 2" 2 3 2 3 2 2" 2 3 2 3 2 2" 1 2

Ex. 4.20

6+ 5 4 5 4 4' 4+ 3' 2 3' 2

Ex. 4.21

6+ 5 4 5 4 4' 4 5 4 4 5 4 4+ 3' 2

Ex. 4.22 (Track 44)

4 5 4 6+ 5 4 4 5 4 4+ 3' 2

Ex. 4.23

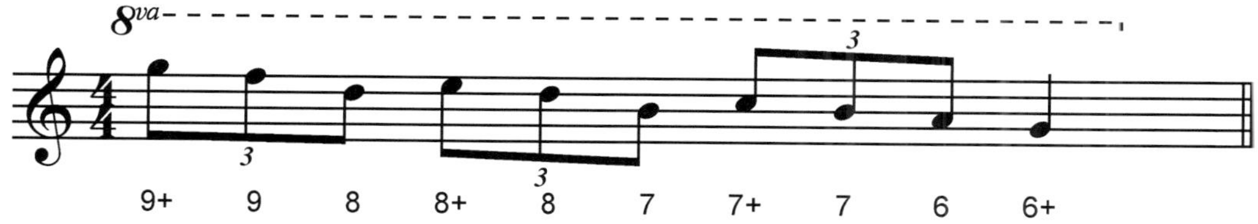

Ex. 4.24

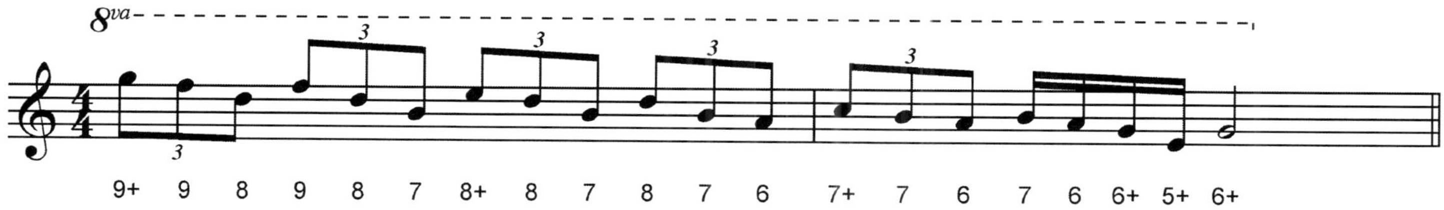

Ex. 4.25

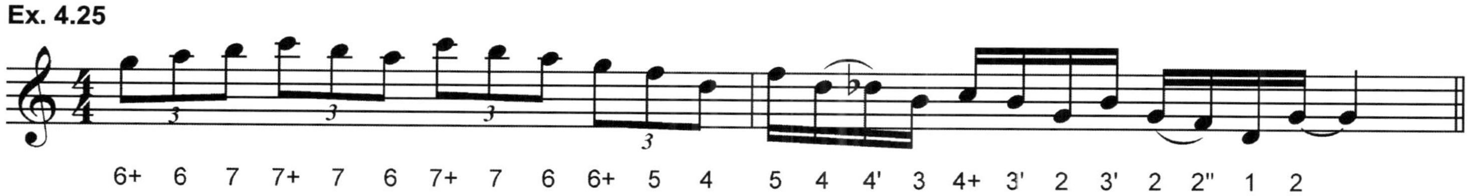

Ex. 4.26

Our last example mixes the high-end lick from Ex. 4.23 with Ex. 4.21. You can hear that the goal here is to experiment with different ranges and connect them together to make long, fluid lines on the harp.

Words of Caution

The longer you play fast, the higher the probability that you'll drift out of time. To check if you're playing in time play to a jam track and record yourself playing fast runs. Slow your recording down with a program like the Amazing Slow Downer and you'll be able to hear whether your licks are staying in time with the music. When it's slowed down, what you're playing should make musical sense and sound good. Many players play fast for the sake of playing fast—and when you slow it down you can hear that what they play makes no musical sense. You of course don't want to be one of those players!

Your best bet to stay in time and to not strain the listener's ears with a barrage of fast licks 100% of the time—ANY good technique will sound bad when over-used—is to play with bursts of speed. Play some killer notes with nice tone or texture and then launch into a fast combination of notes. Mixing it up is the key to not running out of ideas too soon, to staying in time, and to keeping it fresh for the listener.

Homework

The most difficult aspect of playing speed licks is to place them into the context music... especially with good rhythm. Play these licks to the various chord progression backing tracks I've provided on the recorded CD. Again, most importantly record yourself jamming to these tracks and listen back to them, focusing on whether you're playing in time.

Chapter 5 – **Power Licks**

The guitarist on the recording which accompanies this book is John Garcia. John is a master of the extended solo—he can easily wow the crowd for twenty choruses. Not only does he own a huge vocabulary of licks, he's also very adept at scale combinations and arpeggios at lightning speed. My playing, on the other hand, has become more and more classic in nature over the years. In my teens my focus was on playing fast and extended runs that traversed the entire range of the harmonica; but that has given way to an emphasis on tone and repetitive phrasing influenced by jump and swing blues—very much in the vein of Little Walter, George "Harmonica" Smith and those that followed in their footsteps. Speed is no longer my strength—it could be, with focused practice, but it just isn't my cup of tea any more.

So... how does this classic blues harmonica player take a solo after John Garcia? The obvious choice is the approach of intensity. Fast runs are intense and powerful—but so are heavy textures and an intense vibrato. This approach is also a hugely important tool for Rock harmonica players. Not only do Rock players focus on speed and bluesy notes, they focus on thick, powerfully presented licks!

The first step in the pursuit of intensity is to realize that the harmonica's greatest strength is in its ability to present a note in so many different textures. This is the key: texture. Let's take the simple lick below as an example.

Ex. 5.1 – Basic Lick (Track 45)

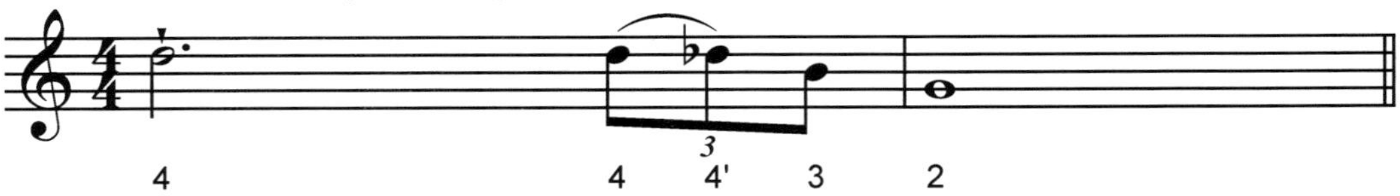

A shake is always a good option for adding texture.

Ex. 5.2 – As a Shake

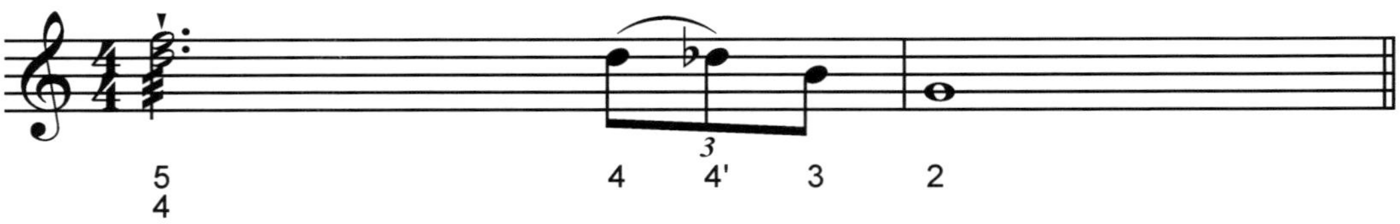

Let's now make it more powerful by adding a little bit of the upper hole—in this case the 5 draw. The more of the 5 draw you add, the nastier it gets!

Ex. 5.3 – With 5 Draw

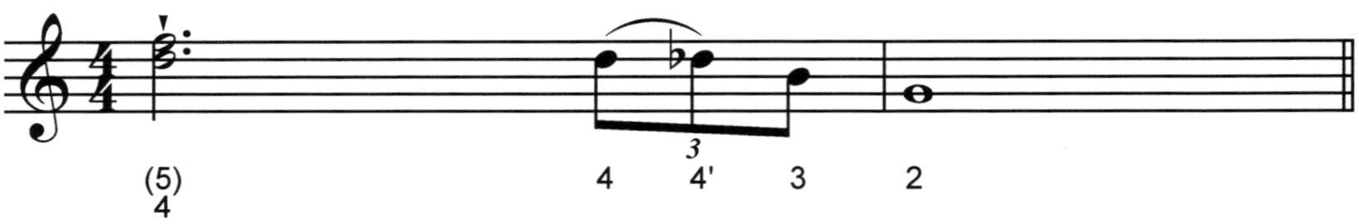

Let's now add vibrato.

Ex. 5.4 – With Vibrato

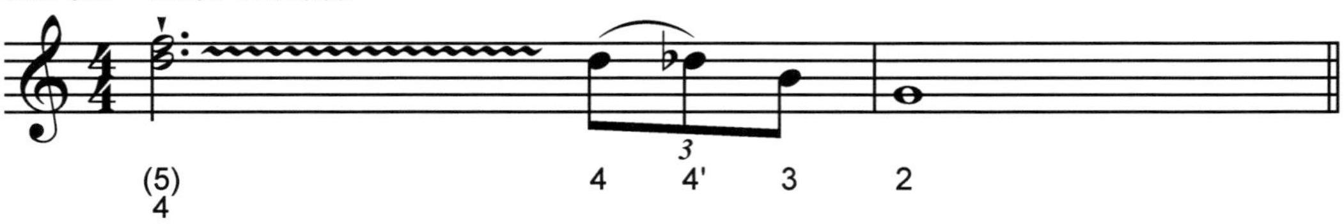

The 3 draw can also be bent down a half step to fit within the blues scale and make it more bluesy.

Ex. 5.5 – With 3' (Track 46)

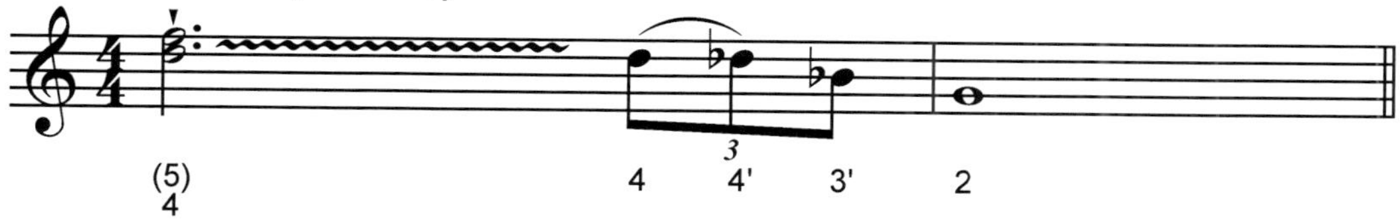

Let's make the 3' thicker by adding a little bit of the 4 draw.

Ex. 5.6 – 3' with 4'

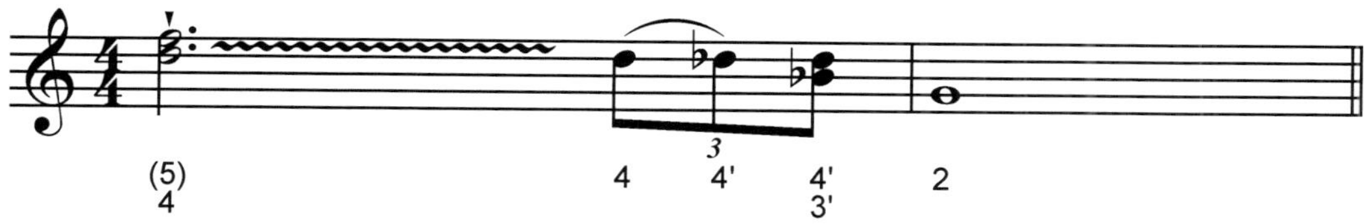

Let's now open our cupped hands on the 4 draw to change its tone.

Ex. 5.7 – Opening Cup

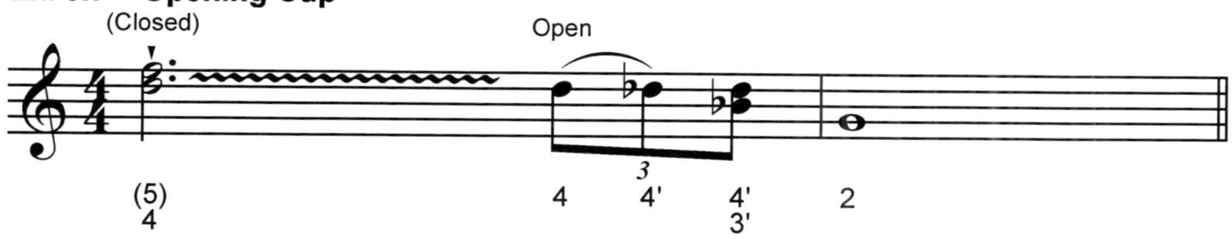

And now let's make it even bigger-sounding by rhythmically (slower than your vibrato) opening and closing your cup to create what I call a double vibrato.

Ex. 5.8 – Opening Cup

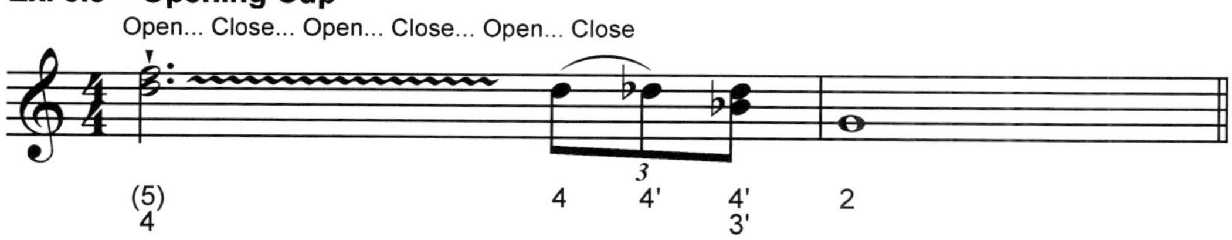

Listening to our starting example (Ex. 5.1) and final version (Ex. 5.8), you'll hear a huge difference in the presentation—and impact—of this lick. Let's now take a lick that can benefit from the textural presentations tongue blocking has to offer. Teaching tongue blocking is not the focus of this book, but it is necessary to mention it here. Here's our basic lick.

Ex. 5.9 – Basic Lick (Track 47 - A Harmonica)

Let's now slap each note. This is where your lips are over four holes and your tongue blocks the holes to the left, leaving the right-most hole open. Each note starts with your tongue off (sounding the chord) as a type of pickup and slaps down (with a light touch) for the single note. Each note has this chord-to-single- note approach.

Ex. 5.10 – With Slaps

Let's now play the last note as a flutter tongue. This is basically a slap, but many times over. It's the alternation of tongue-on (single note) and tongue-off (chord) that gives the flutter tongue its signature pulsating sound.

Ex. 5.11 – With Flutter

If we add a little bit of the 6 draw to your flutter it gets even bigger!

Ex. 5.12 – With Flutter and 6 Bleed

Though not exclusively a tongue block technique, the shake sounds great here as well.

Ex. 5.13 – With Shake

It's hard to deny that the harmonica is amazing in its ability to change the presentation of a passage. Below are some more POWER LICKS to add to your vocabulary. The previous lick could have also used octaves. Our first two examples demonstrate the power of octaves.

Ex. 5.14 (Track 48)

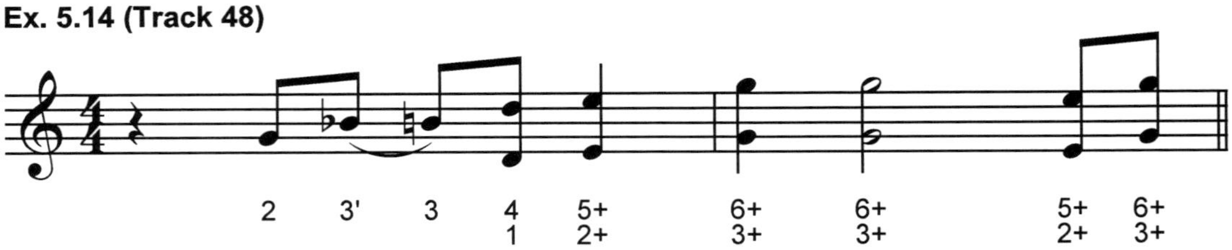

Ex. 5.15

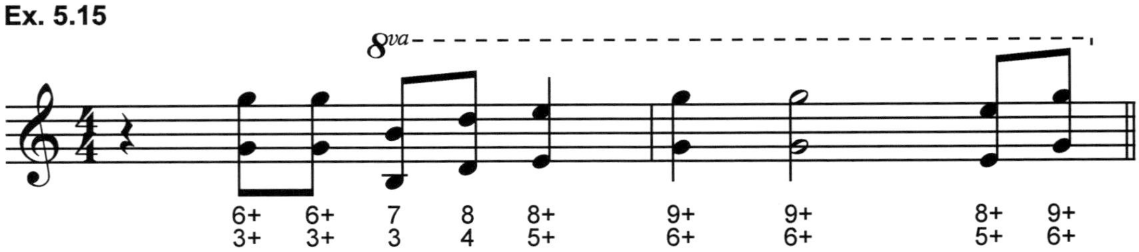

Ex. 5.16 – C Harmonica

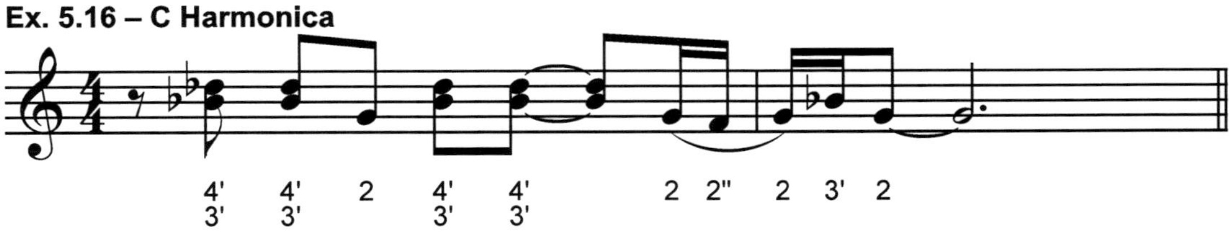

Ex. 5.17

Ex. 5.18

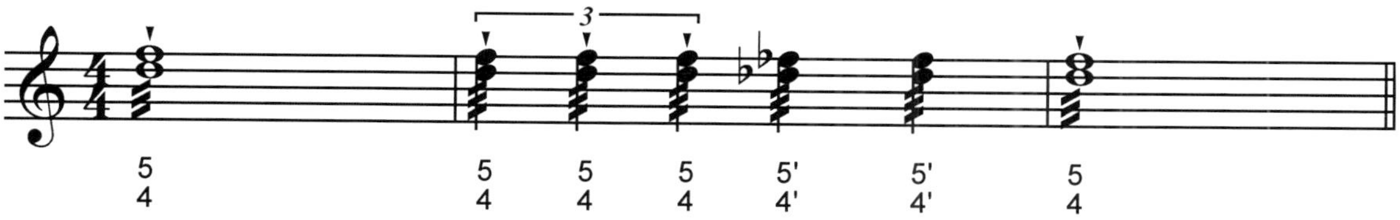

Ex. 5.19

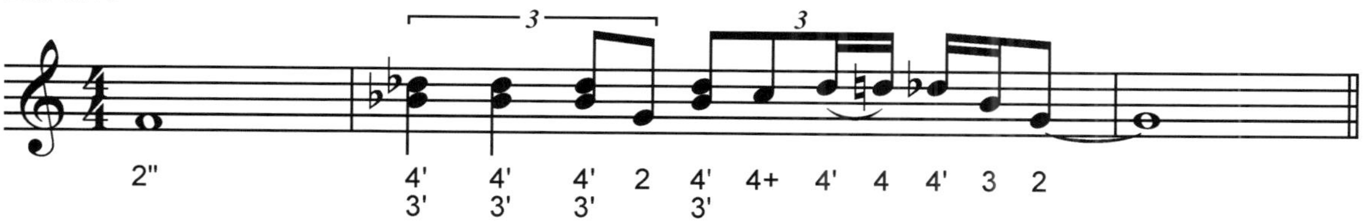

Ex. 5.20

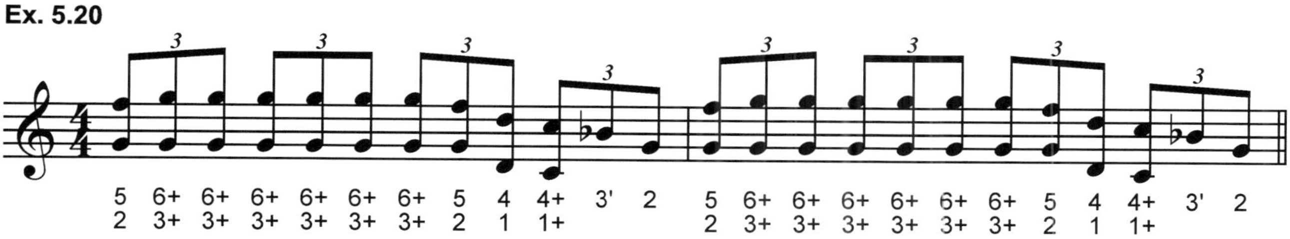

Chapter 6 – **Decoding Music for Improvisation**

Traditional Blues harmonica players focus on developing their soloing vocabulary through studying songs and applying the licks they learn. Rock harmonica players do the same, but due to the fact that every song has a unique chord structure, a rudimentary understanding of scales and chords are essential. Plainly put—players that ignore this part of their music studies are destined to fudge their way through the music… hitting as many notes as they can, hoping that listeners won't notice the notes that don't match. There is a system to this… there's no mystery to it. Take your intuitive skills, the licks you worked so hard to learn, and mix it with a basic understanding of music and you'll be a dangerous player!

We'll start with a general understanding of how scales and chords are built. We'll then apply them to the harmonica.

Scale Theory

The smallest distance between two notes is the ***Half Step*** (also known as a semitone). From these half steps larger intervals, scales and chords are made. Demonstrated below is the chromatic scale from A to A using sharps. This scale can also be constructed using flats (A-sharp turns into B-flat, C-sharp turns into D-flat, etc.)

Ex. 6.1 – Chromatic Scale: A to A (Track 49)

Most music works within the diatonic system. Diatonic denotes a scale that uses two half steps and five whole steps for its construction. A ***Whole Step*** is created when playing two notes separated by two half steps. Our next example demonstrates the A Major scale. The ***Major Mode*** (also known as Ionian) places the half steps between the third and fourth notes in the scale, commonly referred to as ***Scale Degrees***. The second half step occurs between the seventh and eighth scale degrees. This is demonstrated below.

Ex. 6.2 – Major Scale: A to A

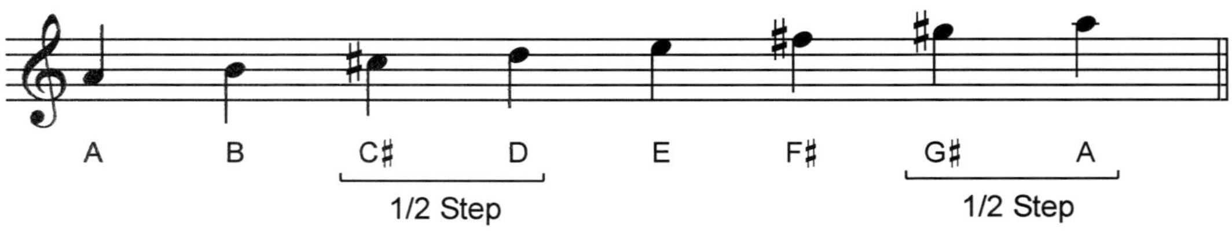

Following this system of whole steps and half steps you can create a major scale starting from any note. The ***Minor Mode*** (also known as Aeolian) places the half steps between the second and third scale degrees and the fifth and sixth scale degrees. This ***A Minor*** scale is demonstrated below.

Ex. 6.3 – Minor Scale: A to A

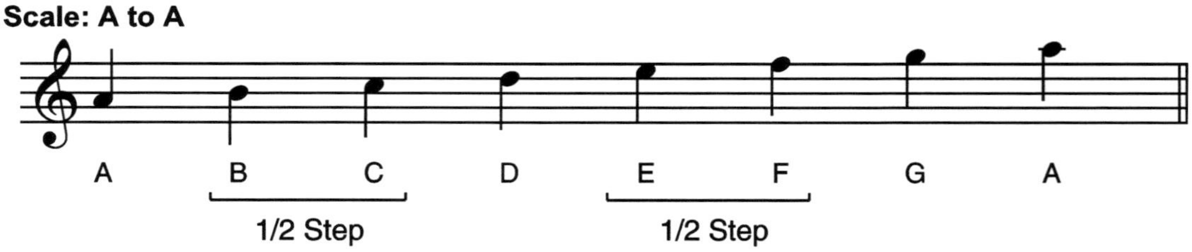

From these scales, melodies can be made.

Chord Theory

This is our main focus for understanding music theory. If the band plays the **IV** (four) Chord, we need to be able to identify the notes that are in that chord so we can play them as well so we match—to sound good. To build a chord, start with a note from the scale and build in thirds. Let's use a C scale as an example. The numbers below the notes designate their position in the scale (scale degree).

Ex. 6.4 – C Major Scale (Track 50)

To make a **I** Chord, start with the first note of the scale (position 1) and build in thirds. Skip the D and play the E, skip the F and play G, and stop. The **I** Chord notes are **C E G**. **C** is the **Root** of the chord. **E** is the **Third** of the chord (third note from the root). **G** is the **Fifth** of the chord. You can continue up the chord, but let's stick with what is called a ***Triad*** (grouping of three notes in thirds). This is demonstrated below.

Ex. 6.5 – I Chord

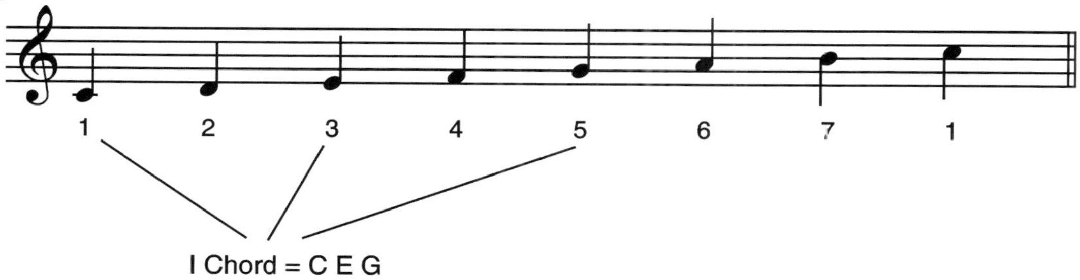

Following the same procedure for all of the notes will give you all seven chords. This is demonstrated below with the **C Major Scale**.

Ex. 6.6 – C Major Scale Chords

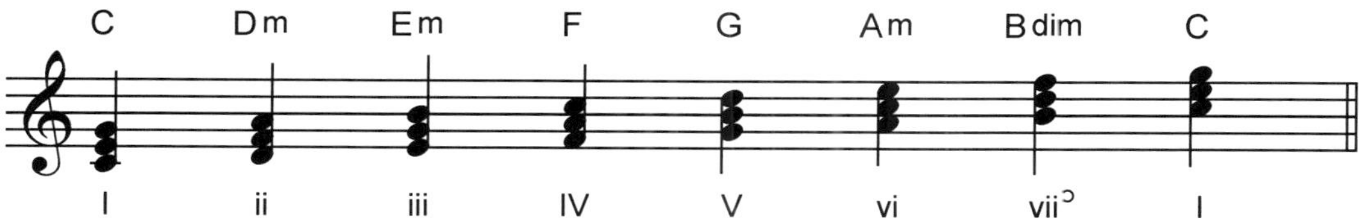

The same can be done with any other diatonic scale. Demonstrated below is the **A Minor Scale** we looked at before with its chords.

Ex. 6.7 – A Minor Scale

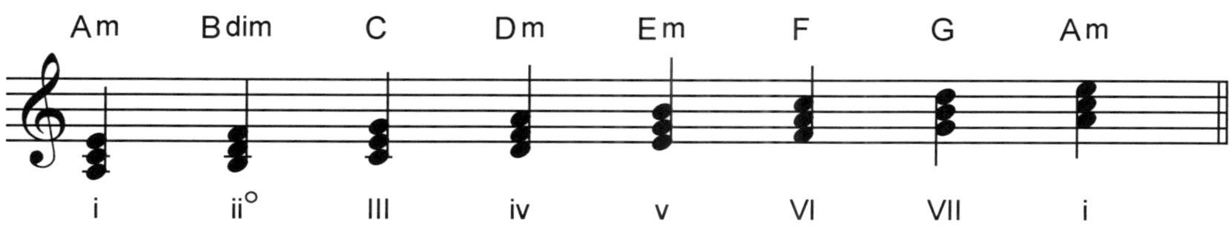

Chord Qualities

Under each of the chords from the previous examples (Ex. 6.6 and 6.7) there are ***Roman Numerals*** representing their chord qualities. Upper case Roman numeral (**I**) represents a ***Major Chord***. A lower case Roman numeral (**i**) represents a ***Minor Chord***. A lower case Roman numeral with a small circle (**i°**) represents a ***Diminished Chord***. An upper case Roman numeral with a small plus (**I⁺**) represents an ***Augmented Chord***. All of these chords, though built from the same root note in thirds, have quite a different sound to them; this is called the chord quality. The chord quality is determined by the interval between each of the notes. The interval we use is that of thirds.

A minor third is built from three half steps.

Ex. 6.8 – Minor 3rd

A major third is built from four half steps.

Ex. 6.9 – Major 3rd

All of the chord qualities are built from either major or minor thirds. Demonstrated below are all of the chords and the intervals they use.

Ex. 6.10 – Chord Qualities (Track 51)

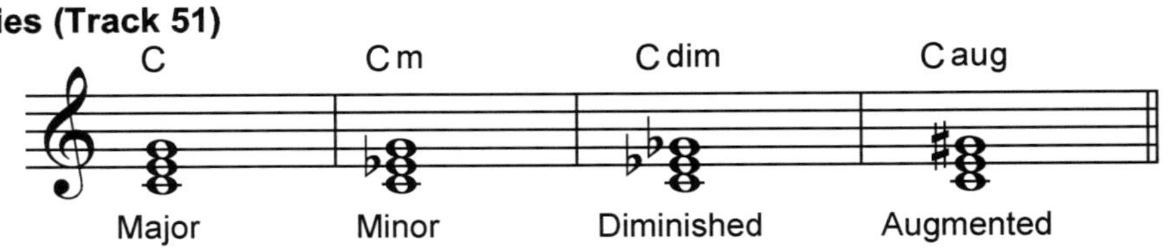

A major chord uses a major third (C to E) with a minor third on top (E to G). Minor uses a minor third with a major third on top. Diminished uses all minor thirds. Augmented uses all major thirds.

Memorize the chord qualities for each of the chords found in major and minor (Ex. 6.6 and 6.7). Listen to the recording and train your ear to hear the differences between the chord qualities; this will help in your soloing to decipher chord changes quicker and more accurately.

Now that you understand how to build in thirds, we can go beyond the basic triad into what Blues and Rock will commonly use.

7th Chords

The 7th chord (chord with the seventh scale degree added) is the bread and butter of Blues and Rock. Detailed below are the common forms of the 7th chord used. Be aware that the most common Dominant 7th Chord also goes by the name of Major-Minor 7th, or more simply just a 7th.

Ex. 6.11 – 7th Chords

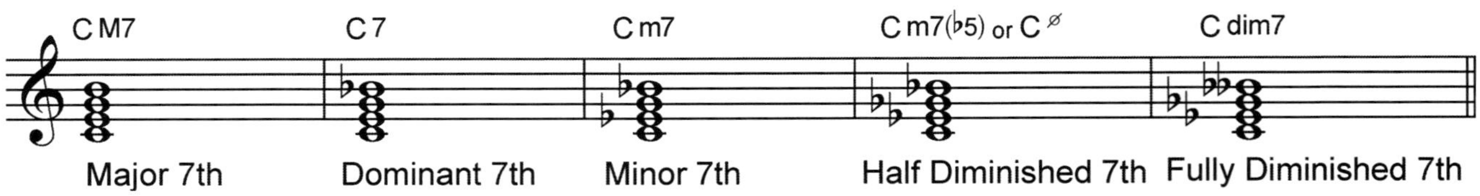

9th Chords

9th chords (chord with the ninth scale degree added, also known as the second) add a nice texture to the often over-used 7th chords. The various 9th chords are demonstrated below; notice some of the chords include or exclude the 7th. The 9th and minor 9th are the most common.

Ex. 6.12 – 9th Chords

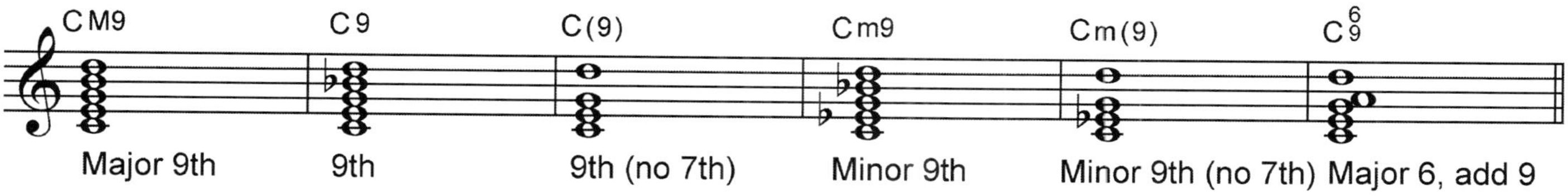

Arpeggios & Chord Scales

Each of the chords we have defined has scales that work well with them for soloing. Let's take a moment to look at a standard twelve bar blues progression and see what chord scale is commonly used. The twelve-bar blues progression uses the **I7**, **IV7** and **V7** Chords. This is demonstrated below in the key of G.

Ex. 6.13 – Twelve Bar Blues

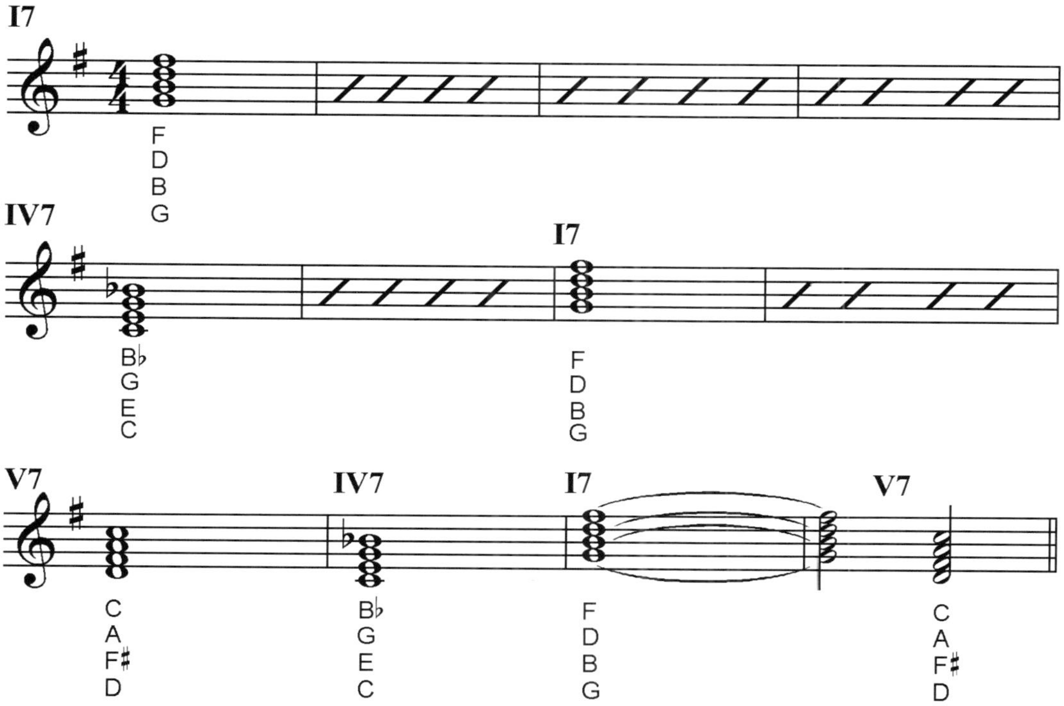

It makes sense that when the band plays a chord, the soloist should also play notes of the chord if he or she wants to match. True, but there are other notes that work as well. Let's start with the ones that match the most. We can then venture off to other notes that also work. Our next example plays each note of the chord arpeggiated (one note after another).

Ex. 6.14 – Arpeggios (Track 52)

Knowing the notes of each chord used in a song is your first step to being able to solo. Play each chord tone from the lowest note in your range to the highest note in your range. This is called playing the ***Arpeggio*** of the chord. By memorizing a chord's arpeggio within the full range of your instrument, you know what notes can be played as you're playing within any range that a solo may take you.

The Making of a Chord Scale

When a note of the scale is used that is not part of the chord (***Non-Chord Tone***), but is used between notes of a chord (***Chord Tones***), it is called a ***Passing Tone***. When a chord tone is played, followed by a non-chord tone one scale step up or down, then returns, the non-chord tone note is called a ***Neighbor Tone***. Passing tones and neighbor tones are the simplest and most commonly used non-chord tones. This is demonstrated below with the **G** chord. "PT" designates the passing tone and "NT" designates the neighbor tone.

Ex. 6.15 – Passing & Neighbor Tones (Track 53, C Harmonica)

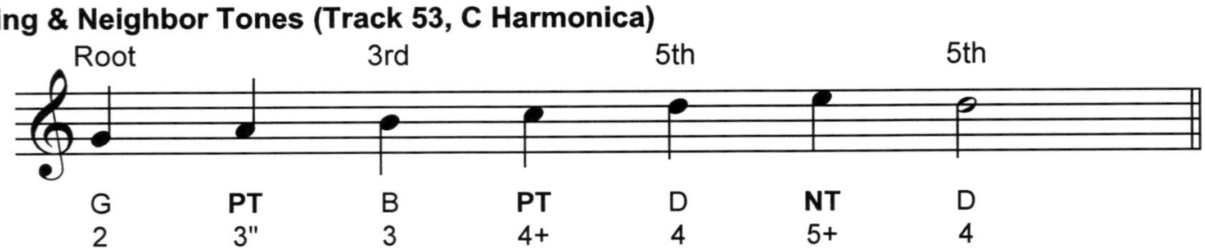

If you use passing tones between each chord tone of a 7th chord, a scale is made. This is demonstrated below with the **G7** Chord.

Ex. 6.16 – Mixolydian Scale

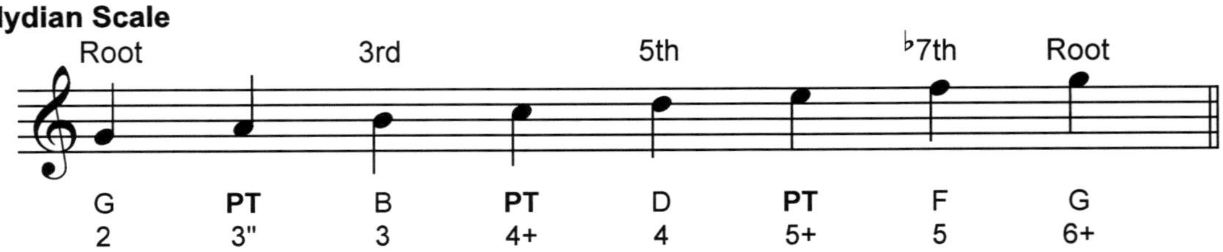

The chord tones with notes added to fill in the holes make the **Mixolydian Scale** (also known as a Dominant Seventh Scale). Notice that the Mixolydian scale is the same as a major scale with a lowered 7th. Any of the notes from this scale can be used when soloing, but keep in mind that chord tones are the best notes to hold. The non-chord tones that made the rest of the Mixolydian scale will sound dissonant if played on the beat or held for too long. This is fine if you're building tension (that's a good thing—music is built on tension and release), but keep in mind it needs to be resolved to a chord tone or root note if you want to finish the phrase. Demonstrated below is an example in G with the **I7**, **IV7** and **V7** Chords and their corresponding Mixolydian Scales. **I7** uses the G Mixolydian scale, **IV7** uses the C Mixolydian scale, and **V7** uses the D Mixolydian scale.

Ex. 6.17 **I7**

G	**PT**	B	**PT**	D	**PT**	F	G
2	3"	3	4+	4	5+	5	6+

IV7

C	**PT**	E	**PT**	G	**PT**	B♭	C
1+	1	2+	2"	2	3"	3'	4+

V7

D	**PT**	F#	**PT**	A	**PT**	C	D
1	2+	2'	2	3"	3	4+	4

Notice that all of our most common chords are Major—and remember that one of the main elements of Rock music is its use of other chords. Our most common "other" chords are the **ii7** and **vi7** Chords. Below are the chords and chord scales for these. If you're keen with music theory you'll notice the **ii7** Chord is a **IV6** Chord (a **IV** Chord with a major 6th)—this allows us to think of this as a **IV** Chord, which is a chord we're more familiar with. This also allows us to use first position (straight harp) ideas with an emphasis on the 6th. This same thought process applies to the **vi7** Chord. The **vi7** Chord can be thought of as a **I6** Chord, and we can play second position (cross harp) ideas with an emphasis on the 6th.

Ex. 6.18 **ii7**

A	**PT**	C	**PT**	E	**PT**	G	A
3"	3	4+	4	5+	NA	6+	6

vi7

E	**PT**	G	**PT**	B	**PT**	D	E
2+	2'	2	3"	3	4+	4	5+

The most important task when dealing with a new song is to identify the non-standard chords. The standard chords—the most common chords used for Blues, Rock and Pop from all eras—are **I**, **IV** and **V.** With any other chords, it's best to focus on playing the chord tones. Wait for the standard, more familiar, chords and go to town on them!

I've made two charts for you that you'll find immensely useful once you've figured out the chords of a given song. These show the notes that match for each given chord. Be aware that your bending has to be spot on if you choose to play a bent note. If your bending is still developing, choose a non-bent note if you want it to sound good.

Our first chart shows all of the notes for our standard chords in major. This is based on playing in second position. For the major chords if you play the note in parentheses it will make the chord minor. For the minor chords if you play the note in parentheses it will make the chord major.

Standard Chords in Major

I7	ii7	iii7	IV7	V7	vi7	viii7
10'+ (10"+)	10 / 10+	10	10"+ / 10+	10 / 10+	10'+	10 / 10+ (10"+)
9 / 9+	9+	9'+	9+	9'+ (9)	9+	9'+
8	8+	8 (8'+)	8+ (8'+)	8	8+ / 8	8'+ / 8+
7	7+	7	7+	7+	7	7+
6+	6+ / 6	6	6+	6	6+ (6')	6
5	5+	-	5+	(5)	5+	5+
4	4+ (4')	4	4+	4+ / 4	4	4+ (4')
3+ / 3 (3')	3+ / 3"	3" / 3	3+ / 3'	3"	3+ / 3 (3"')	3" (3')
2" / 2	2+ / 2	2'	2+ / 2	2' (2")	2+ / 2	2+ / 2'
1	1+ (1')	1	1+	1+ / 1	1	1+ (1')

Our second chart shows all of the notes for our non-standard chords. You'll notice that your options are much more limited and what is available can be difficult to play. These chords do not work to the strengths of the harmonica. Again, for the major chords if you play the note in parentheses it will make the chord minor. For the minor chords if you play the note in parentheses it will make the chord major.

Non-Standard Chords in Major

Flat-ii7	Flat-iii7	Flat-V7	Flat-vi7	Flat-viii7
10'+ (10+)	10"+	10'+	10"+	(10) / (10+)
9'+	9	9 (9'+)	9'+ (9+)	9
8'+	(8)	-	8'+	8'+
7 (7+)	-	7	-	7 (7+)
6'	6'	6'	(6+)	6' (6)
-	5	5	-	5
(4+)	4' (4)	4'	4'	4+
3"' / 3	3"' / 3'	3"' / 3	(3+) 3'	3"' / 3 (3")
2'	2"	2" (2+)	2' (2)	2"
(1+)	1' (1)	1'	1'	(1+)

Homework

The next chapter will teach you the common chord progressions used in Rock. For each chord in a progression list all of the notes from the above charts next to each chord so that you can easily see what notes will match (the notes you can hold on and will sound good). Keep in mind that playing these "matching" notes only will be boring.

Use a combination of chords tones that you know match (charts above), scales that you know will sound good (Major Pentatonic Scale for light songs and Blues Scale for bluesy songs) and of course the lick vocabulary you've worked so hard on developing over the years (your study of great songs).

Earmark this page—you'll be referencing these charts all the time!

Chapter 7 – **Common Chord Progressions**

Traditional blues harmonica players develop their soloing vocabulary through studying songs. When they go to improvise they pull licks from this vocabulary. The challenging aspect of Rock is that each song you play will use different chords, or at the very least use common chords in a different order. In this chapter we'll dig into different chord progressions and how to deal with them using the information we've studied so far. It's very important that you take the time to list under each chord what hole numbers on the harmonica match (information found on the previous page's charts).

We'll start with the good ol' **12 Bar Blues Progression**. For each chord I present you with the notes that can be played on the lower holes of the harmonica. I'm using the chart I provided for you in Chapter 6. I recommend you spend time on the high-end as well: use the same chart in Chapter 6 and add those notes to the list. For each example track you'll first hear the play-along; then me playing the chord tones as presented below; and lastly me improvising to the same progression.

Ex. 7.1 – 12 Bar Blues (Track 54, C Harmonica)

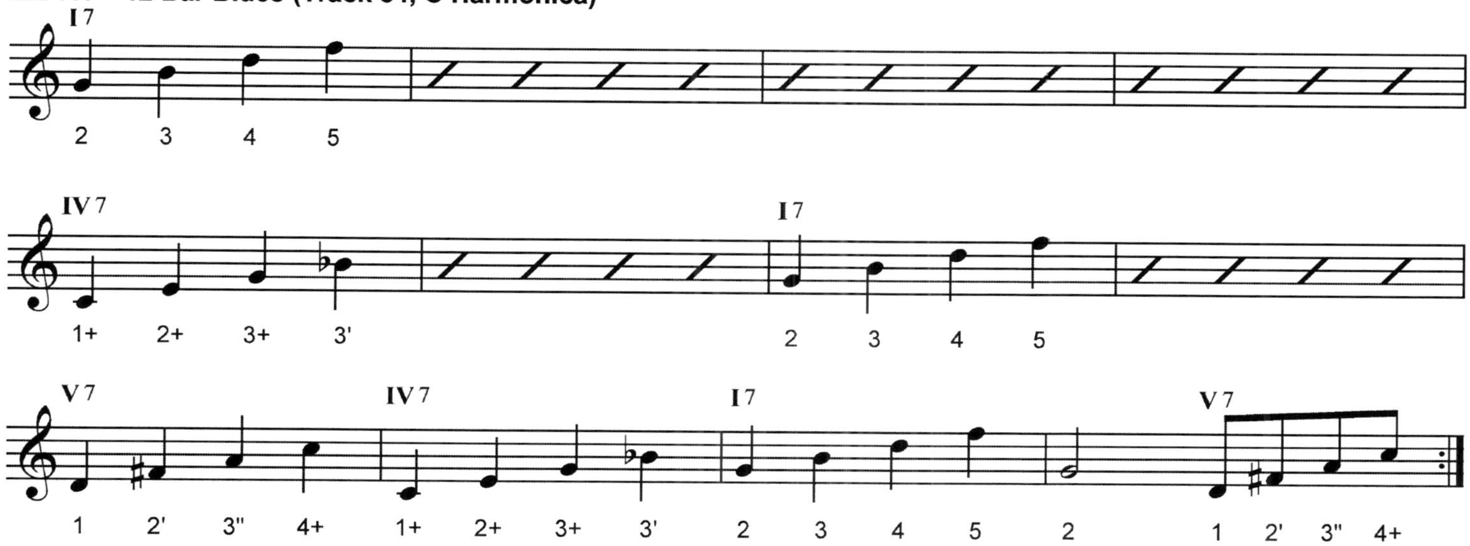

Here's the same progression with the addition of a **Quick Change**. The quick change makes measure two a **IV** Chord.

Ex. 7.2 – 12 Bar Blues w/Quick Change (Track 55, C Harmonica)

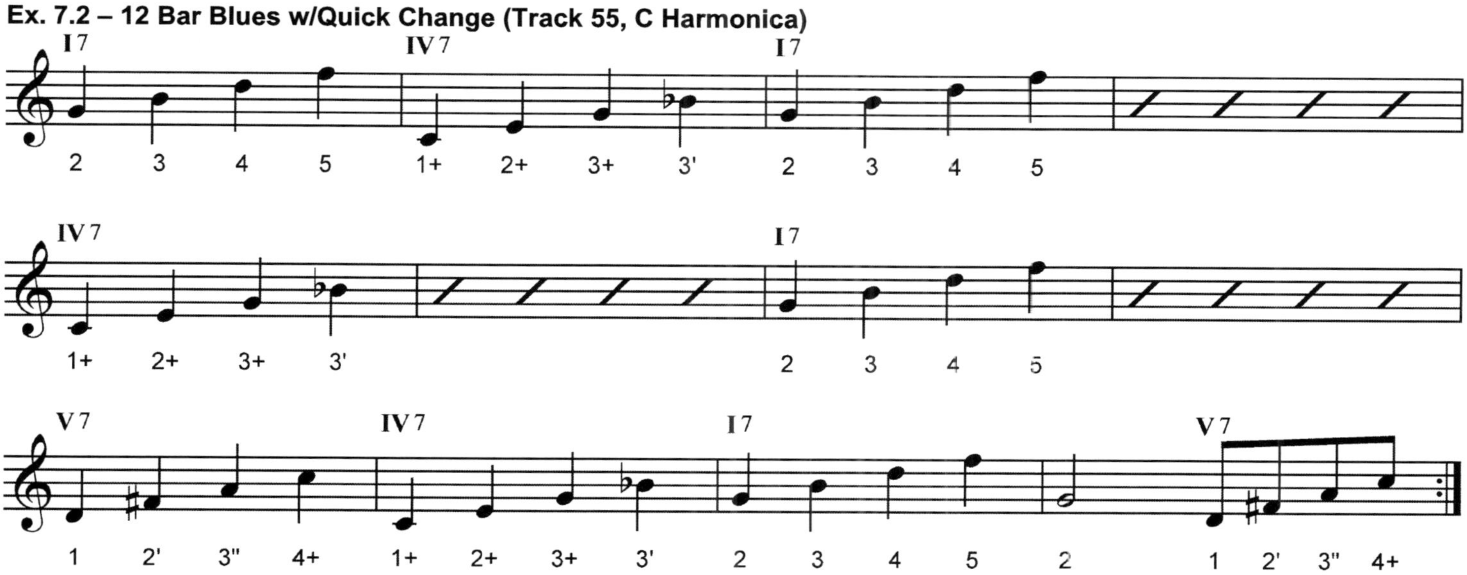

Here's the **16 Bar Blues** pattern. This is the same as the 12 Bar Blues Progression with the opening measures of **I** Chord doubled from four to eight.

Ex. 7.3 – 16 Bar Blues (Track 56, C Harmonica)

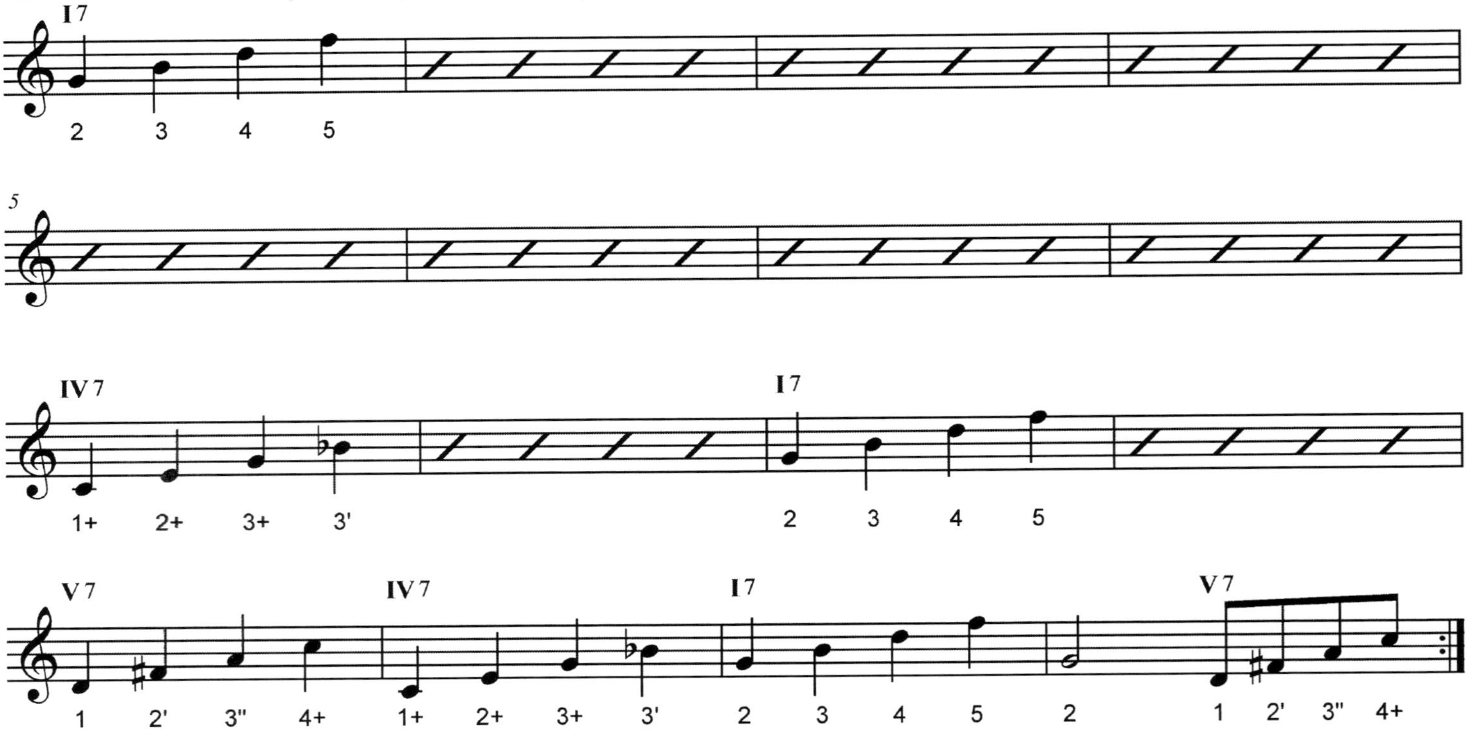

Let's now take a look at some two bar progressions that use the **I**, **IV** and **V** Chords for their construction. Example 7.4 is a progression in the Hendrix vein. This groove has a dark feel, so the 3rd has been omitted; you'll most likely want to emphasize the flat-3rd to match the more bluesy nature of this progression. A good way to approach improvising to these examples is to pick one note per chord and hit it, tipping your hat to the chord change, allowing your improvising to say the rest after that. Again, remember that you can use the blues scale as your focus and to a certain degree ignore chord change.

Ex. 7.4 – A Harmonica (Track 57)

Example 7.5 is a progression similar to what you hear in "La Bamba;" and Example 7.6 is similar to that of "Wild Thing." The major pentatonic scale is a good choice here.

Ex. 7.5 – C Harmonica (Track 58)

Ex. 7.6 – A Harmonica (Track 59)

Here are three more two-bar progressions. Example 7.7 uses the **II** Chord; example 7.8 uses the **Flat-VII** Chord; and example 7.9 uses a minor **i** Chord along with the **Flat-VII** and **Flat-VI** Chords (similar to what you hear on "Stray Cat Strut," "Walk Don't Run" and some Flamenco tunes). We'll again avoid major-3rds for this last example since our first chord is minor. The blues scale is again a great choice for Examples 7.8 and 7.9.

Ex. 7.7 – C Harmonica (Track 60)

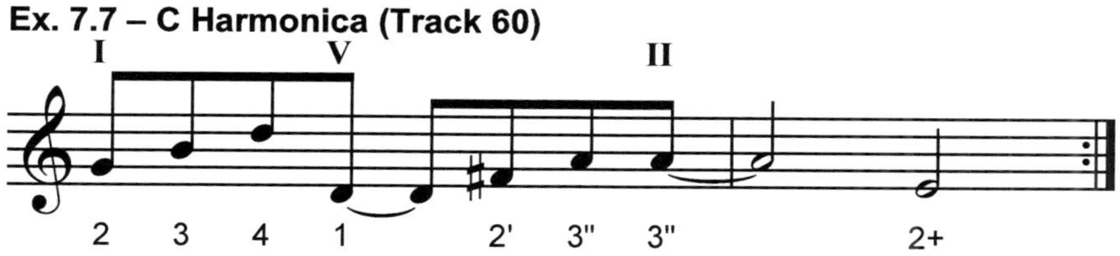

Ex. 7.8 – A Harmonica (CD2, Track 1)

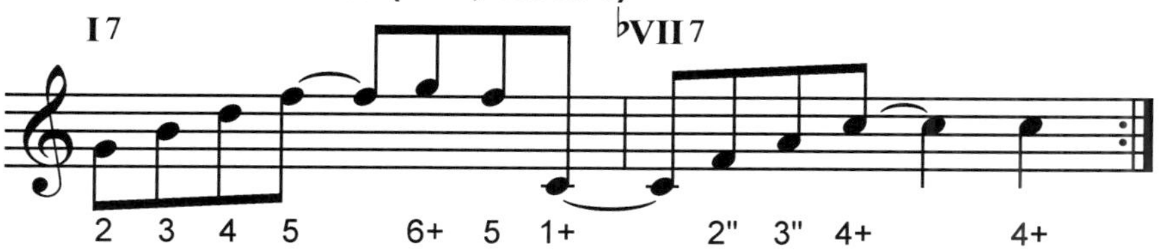

Ex. 7.9 – C Harmonica (CD2, Track 2)

Our next two examples are four bars in length. Example 7.10 is the type of progression you hear on Hendrix's "Hey Joe." This progression is unique in that the chords cycle in fifths (E-flat, B-flat, F, C and finally G). Example 7.11 is what's commonly known as a Two-Note Rock.

Ex. 7.10 – A Harmonica (CD2, Track 3)

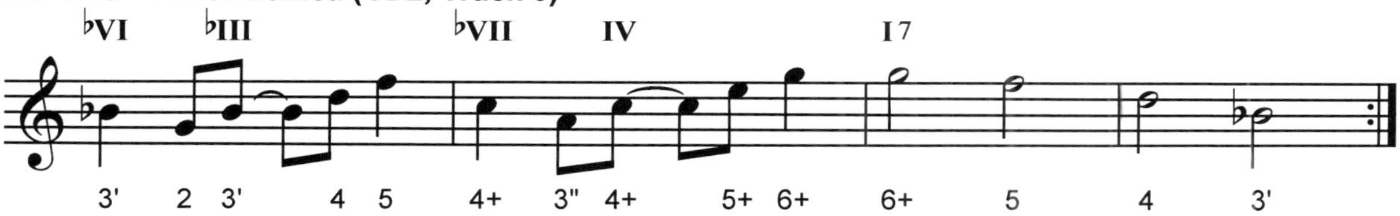

Ex. 7.11 – A Harmonica (CD2, Track 4)

Both of these progressions are unique in the fact that from chord to chord there are notes in common as well as a very cool bass line. Let's examine this using Example 7.11. The first two chords have the D in common and the last two chords have C in common. This is shown in Example 7.12.

Ex. 7.12 – A Harmonica (CD2, Track 5)

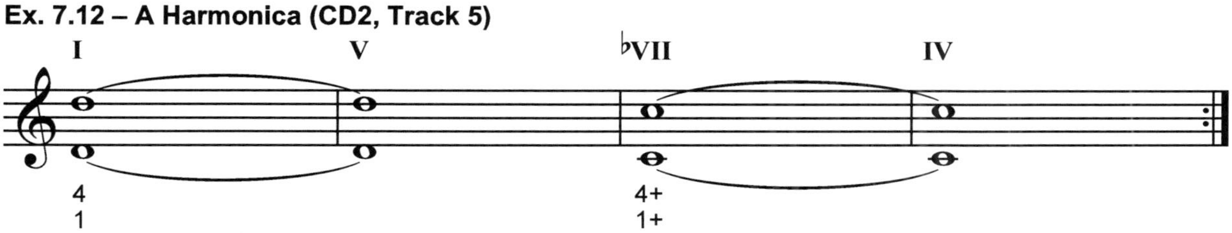

The bass line is even cooler. If you start with the 2 draw for the **I** Chord (root), and then play 2' for the **V** Chord (3rd), then the 2" for the **Flat-VII** Chord (root) and finally the 2+ for the **IV** Chord (3rd), you get this great descending passage that moves in half steps (chromatically). This is shown in Example 7.13.

Ex. 7.13 – A Harmonica

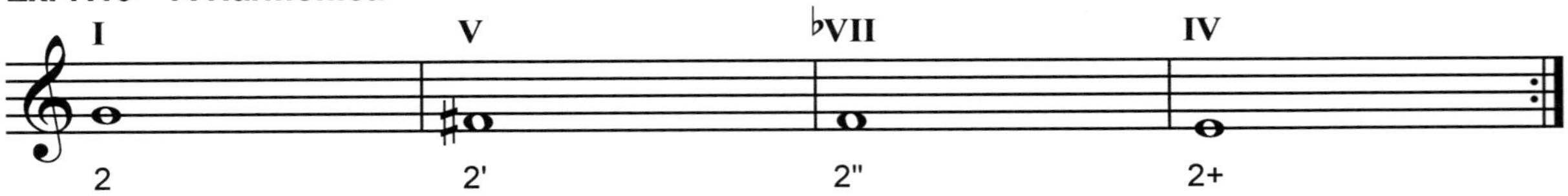

If you take the time to look at each chord and also look at how it relates to the chords around it, you'll find great melodic opportunities.

Let's finish our examples with some more classic chord progressions. Example 7.14 is an eight bar progression that we see in Rock and some Rock-based Blues. Example 7.15 is a twelve bar blues, but mixes the chords around a bit; "I Hear You Knocking" is a great example of this chord progression. Finally we finish with the super-classic Blues-based Rock progression in Example 7.16, the twelve bar blues with a long **V** (**V** Chord is played for two measures—measures 9 and 10).

Ex. 7.14 – A Harmonica (CD2, Track 6)

Ex. 7.15 – C Harmonica (CD2, Track 7)

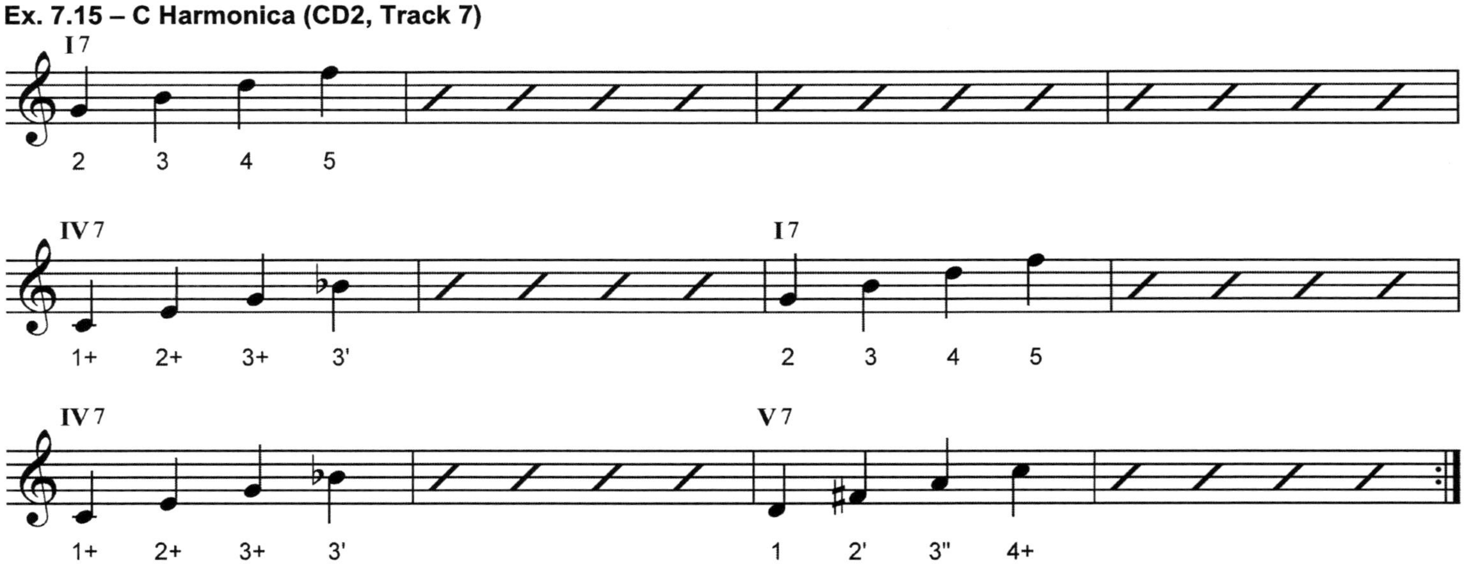

Ex. 7.16 – A Harmonica (CD2, Track 8)

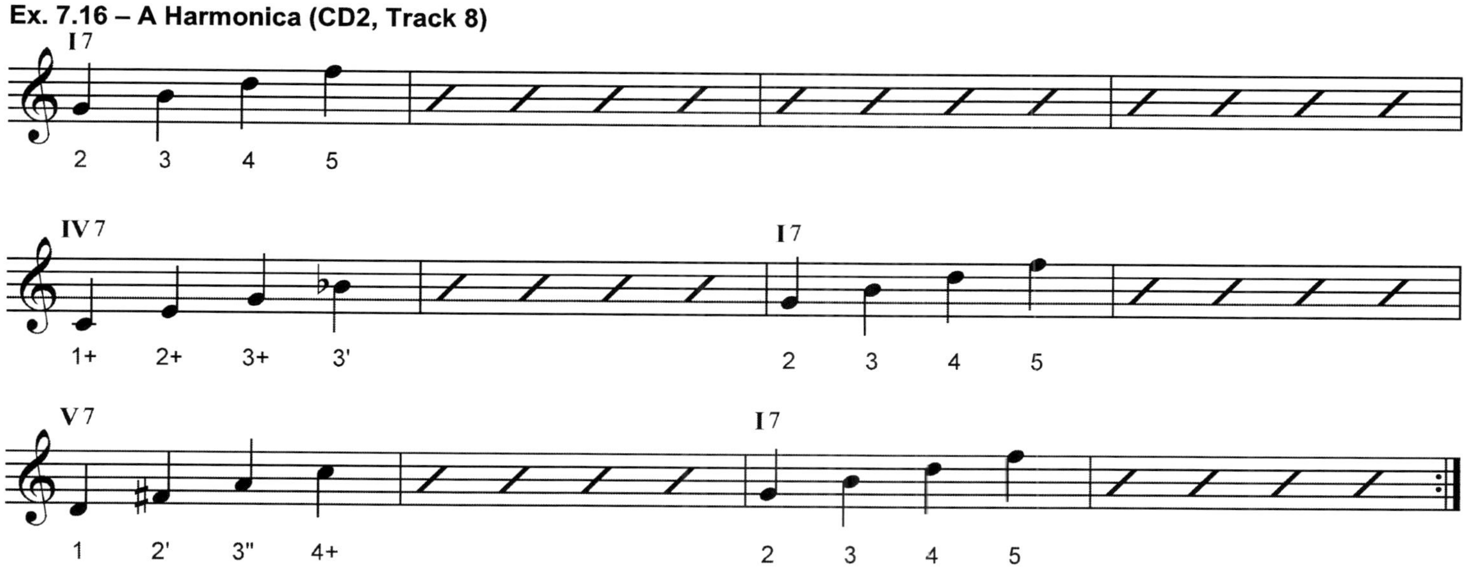

Homework

Spend a good week on each progression presented in this chapter. Mix chord tones, scales and lick vocabulary together to make an interesting solo. THIS TAKES TIME. You'll most likely not be happy with what you come up with your first run through... keep working it!

I recommend coming back to this chapter every year for many years to come. Each year you'll come back with more lick vocabulary and the musicianship that a year's growth has to offer. Take your time… enjoy the lifelong journey that takes to become a great harmonica player.

Chapter 8 – **Hooks, Heads & Sequences**

Head

The ***Head*** is constructed the same as any other chorus, but it's the most melodic and catchy of all choruses, making it the main theme/melody of a song. The head is commonly played at the opening of a song, unless an intro is present. Many times the head is repeated for a total of two choruses in the opening. Though there are examples of great songs with a head that never returns after the opening (Little Walter instrumentals are great examples of this), most songs will come back to the head at the end. This helps to cement the head (your main theme for the song) into the listener's mind and also helps to tell them the song is coming to a close.

For both the head (and the hook) it's very common for guitar and harmonica to play it together in unison to add weight to this important structural element. Our general rule of thumb is if the head or hook is playable on the harmonica, we play it. Below is an example of a head that the guitar and harmonica play in unison together. This comes from the title track from my CD with John Garcia "Serious Fun."

Ex. 8.1 – A Harmonica (CD2, Track 9)

Hooks & Sequences

How do you approach a song that's hook-driven? It might be a modal tune where there are no chord changes (the song stays on the **I** Chord the whole time) and typical vocal rest areas (where you would fill) are not there. Maybe it's a tune with standard chord changes, but the hook is so strong that when playing anything else it sounds like you're not matching the feel of the band.

The answer is simple. If there's a dominant hook in the song—play it! The ***Hook*** is a small lick (commonly one measure in length, sometimes two) that repeats throughout a song (usually for every verse and chorus). If the hook is one measure in length, it will commonly be sequenced over all the chord changes (the line is transposed up or down to match the **IV** and **V** Chord). The hook can be part of the groove (played by most of the members in the rhythm section) or just played at the opening of particular sections of a song or between the vocals. Like a song with a recognizable head, if a song uses a hook, the hook is the recognizable element in that song. In many cases it's important that you play the hook. For example: if the hook is primarily played by the guitarist in a four-piece band (drums, bass, guitar and you—harp), when the guitar solos, you're expected to continue playing the hook while they solo. Otherwise, the main element of the song disappears during the guitar solo.

Let's start with a simple example of this concept.

Ex. 8.2 – C Harmonica

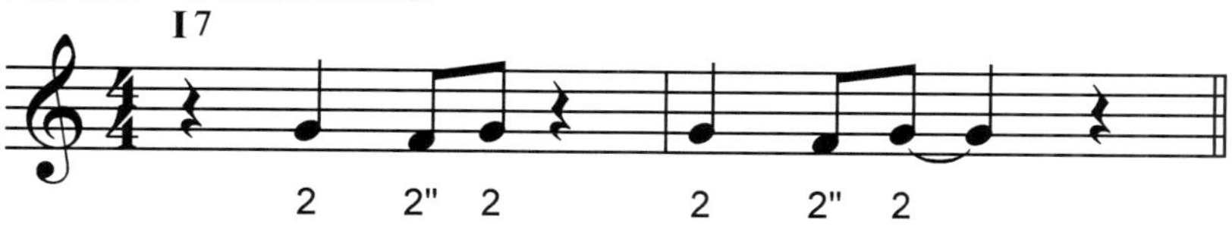

In a blues progression you would hear the band play this hook twice, filling up the first four measures of the **I** Chord. You would then hear the band move this lick up or down to match the **IV** Chord (called a ***Sequence***). Your first task when hearing a song like this is to figure out the hook as first presented on the **I** Chord. I have done this for you in the above example. The task ahead of you is to now figure out where the notes are on your harmonica to play the sequence for the upcoming **IV** Chord. You could do this by ear and maybe get it right. This hook only uses two notes, so you could probably figure it out by ear fairly quickly. But what happens with a lick that's four to five notes long, or when you want to sequence it to the **V** Chord? Using the basic theory studied in Chapter 6 you'll be able to do this. Let's start from the beginning of the process.

Once you've figured out how to play the hook, think about (or write down) what the notes are. Below is an example lick.

Hook:	2	2"	2,	2	2"	2
Pitch:	G	F	G,	G	F	G

You learned in the Chapter 6 that the **I7** Chord is **G—B—D—F**. Your 2 draw (**G**) is the root of the **I7** Chord. Your 2 draw whole step bend (**F**) is the flat-7th of the **I7** Chord. It makes sense that if your hook uses the root and flat-7th of the **I7** Chord, then you would play the root and flat-7th of the **IV7** Chord to create the sequence. That's exactly correct.

The **IV** Chord is **C—E—G—B-flat**. Your root is **C** (found on the 4 blow) and the flat-7th is **B-flat** (found on the 3 draw half step bend). Now that you know the hole numbers, you're ready to go. The following example uses this process to come up with the sequence for both the **IV** and **V** Chords.

Ex. 8.3 – Blues Hook (CD2, Track 10)

Being that the hook was two measures in length, we used the first half of the **V7** Chord sequence (the **V7** Chord at the ninth measure is only one measure long) and the second half of the **IV7** Chord sequence (the **IV7** Chord at the tenth measure is only one measure long as well).

At first you'll need to repeat this process on paper until you have committed the three chords and the C Harmonica note spread to memory. The more you go through this exercise, the quicker you'll become at figuring out the sequence for the other chords in a song when playing with a live band. When I sit in with a band and a song with a hook comes up, I listen carefully to the hook until I have figured it out in my head. When I'm ready I'll start to play the hook with the band (maybe at the second chorus). As I'm playing the **I7** Chord I'm thinking about how to sequence the hook to the **IV7** Chord. As I'm playing the **IV7** Chord I'm thinking about how to sequence the hook to the **V7** Chord.

At first this will be hard to do, but with diligent practice you'll be pleasantly surprised how quickly you can pick up sequences on the spot. Sequences are used a lot.

On the following page I've provided for you a worksheet to use when figuring out sequences. At top left is an example lick that walks you through the process. The next line reminds you of the most common chords. To the right of these chords are the chord scales made from them.

I recommend that you photocopy the following chart and use it every time you need to figure out a sequence. Challenge yourself to listen to the recording for the following examples—figuring out the hook and sequencing the hook to the other chords. Look at the notated examples to see if you were correct.

Be aware that some licks cannot be sequenced to other chords—the harmonica can't play every note in every range of the instrument (your best example of this is that the 3' B-flat played on the **I7** Chord would turn into the note E-flat for **IV7** Chord, which is only available on an 8 blow half step bend). You're guaranteed to find some licks that sound great, some that need rewriting to work, and some that don't work at all or just don't sound good. The key is to experiment!

Sequence Worksheet

Example:

I7	Hole:	3	4	4	5+	4	
	Note:	B	D	D	E	D	
	Degree:	3rd	5th	5th	6th	5th	(Degree of the scale)
IV7	Hole:	5+	6+	6+	6	6+	
	Note:	E	G	G	A	G	
	Degree:	3rd	5th	5th	6th	5th	(Note that the scale degrees stay the same)
V7	Hole:	2'	3"	3"	3	3"	
	Note:	F#	A	A	B	A	
	Degree:	3rd	5th	5th	6th	5th	

Chords & Chord Scales

			1	2	3	4	5	6	♭7	8
I7 =	G B D F	**I7 Scale**	G	A	B	C	D	E	F	G
IV7 =	C E G B♭	**IV7 Scale**	C	D	E	F	G	A	B♭	C
V7 =	D F# A C	**V7 Scale**	D	E	F#	G	A	B	C	D

Worksheet:

I7
Hole: ___ ___ ___ ___ ___ ___ ___ ___ ___ ___ ___ ___ ___ ___
Note: ___ ___ ___ ___ ___ ___ ___ ___ ___ ___ ___ ___ ___ ___
Degree: ___ ___ ___ ___ ___ ___ ___ ___ ___ ___ ___ ___ ___ ___

IV7
Hole: ___ ___ ___ ___ ___ ___ ___ ___ ___ ___ ___ ___ ___ ___
Note: ___ ___ ___ ___ ___ ___ ___ ___ ___ ___ ___ ___ ___ ___
Degree: Same

V7
Hole: ___ ___ ___ ___ ___ ___ ___ ___ ___ ___ ___ ___ ___ ___
Note: ___ ___ ___ ___ ___ ___ ___ ___ ___ ___ ___ ___ ___ ___
Degree: Same

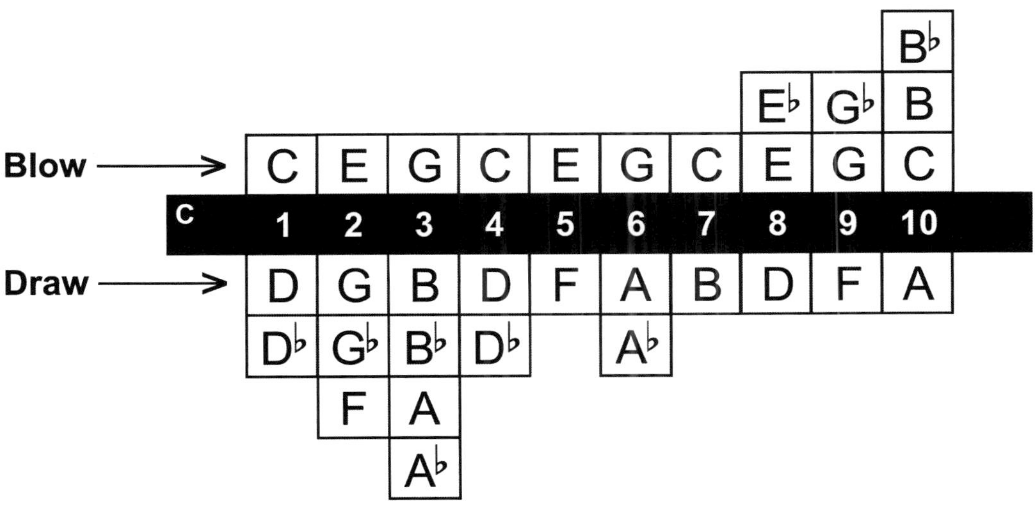

Let's take another example lick and see what it sounds like when sequenced. Below is the **I7** chord version of the hook.

Ex. 8.4 – I7 Lick

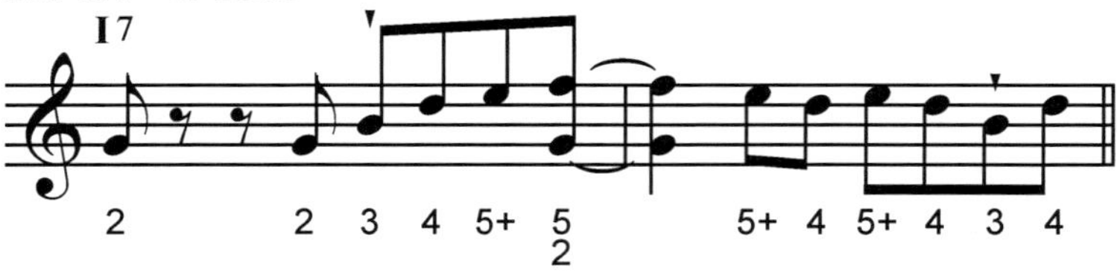

Let's now take a look at sequences for the **IV7** and **V7** Chords. Take note of the change in the sequence at the end of the **IV7** Chord—it's okay to make changes if they benefit the line (in this case the 2" sounds a little more bluesy and sets up the **V7** Chord nicely).

Ex. 8.5 – Full Line with Sequences (CD2, Track 11)

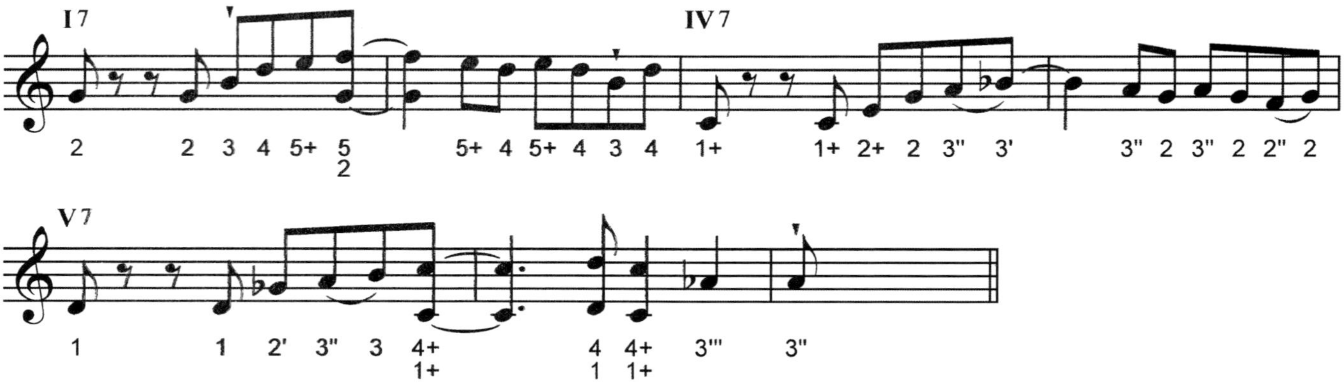

Let's now take a more rockin' example of a hook.

Ex. 8.6 – Rock Hook

Listening to the entire cycle of chords you get the following sequence that needs to be played on the harp. Notice that slight changes have been made to the sequence. After working out a sequence have fun with it—changing it to suit the line and the feel of the music, and working to the strengths of the harmonica.

Ex. 8.7 – Rock Hook Sequence

"Room To Move" by John Mayall is a great example of the use of a hook. In this early Rock classic Mayall plays the hook with the guitar and flute with fills between. Below is a transcription of what he plays on the opening chorus, with some simplification of the line (he used a lot of chord substitutes).

Ex. 8.8 – "Room to Move" (CD2, Track 12 / Play-Along Track on CD2, Track 13)

The hook played on the **I7** Chord is sequenced to the **IV7** Chord, just like we studied above. On the **V7** Chord he leaves the hook to play something else—in this case I think it sounds nice; playing the hook again on the **V** Chord would start to sound a little too redundant.

Special Note About Chords, Hooks & Sequences

I was speaking to my good friend (and respected harmonica educator) Joe Filisko about this book and he reminded me of the solo Norton Buffalo played on Bonnie Raitt's song "Runaway." This is a great example of using the technique of switching harmonicas to play chords that may not sit so well if you were to stay on one harmonica the whole time.

The technique is simple. If you have a **G** chord, then you play the C Harmonica in second position. If it then moves to an **A** chord you grab your D Harmonica and again play in second position. This allows you to avoid foreign chord changes by making them all essentially a **I** Chord in second position.

Peter "Madcat" Ruth is also a player that comes to mind who has used this technique for years, most prominently when playing with the Brubeck family. Visit bluesharmonica.com for an interview where he covers this subject.

Room to Move
Words and Music by John Mayall. ©1969 (Renewed) Unichappell Music Inc.
This Arrangement © 2010 Unichappell Music Inc. All Rights Reserved Including Public Performance.
Used by Permission of Alfred Music Publishing Co., Inc.

Chapter 9 – "Whammer Jammer" Song Study

I asked harmonica players and non-harmonica players what was the most famous song in Rock history to use the harmonica, and they overwhelmingly said "Whammer Jammer" by Magic Dick. So here it is!

"Whammer Jammer" is Magic Dick's (and the band's… this was a group effort) tribute song to the great blues players of the past. You'll notice numerous quotes from famous songs, such as the opening chorus from Rice Miller's "Bye Bye Bird" or turnaround licks from James Cotton's "Creeper." The recorded version I used for the transcription in this book is from the studio (apposed to the live version). The recording I provide for you (this is me playing) is slower than the original. Since the recording is for your study I didn't want speed to get in the way of you learning the song.

Opening (CD2, Track 14)
The opening has a nice flutter tongue on the 5 draw, held until he signals the band for a hit (the symbol above the 5 draw is called a ***Fermata*** and indicates you to hold that as long as you like). In the next lick we see the first of many blow bends. The 10 blow bend can be challenging, make sure to keep your embouchure as small as possible and use the very front of the tongue to achieve this bend. To achieve the vibrato on the 10"+ use a chewing motion. The end of this line (specifically the last two beats) is the pickup to the first chorus.

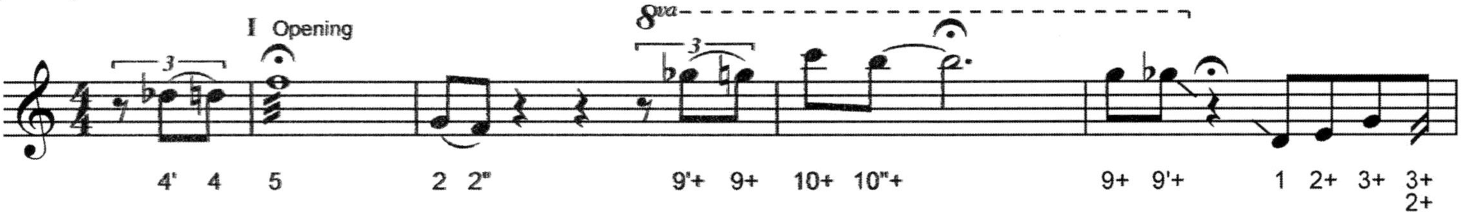

1st Chorus – AAB Chorus Form (CD2, Track 15)
You're all by your lonesome here so make sure that your timing is on. You don't want your audience clapping along and having to stop because you can't play in time. Once you get the licks down, work with a metronome and record yourself to make sure you're staying in rhythm. Experiment with the articulation used on the chords. You could try "TA TA TA TA HU," TA being the draw and HU being the blow. Note the cough (C) he uses on the **V** Chord. Open your lips (if you're tongue blocking just take your tongue off) and cough, not allowing the reeds to vibrate much—it's more of a rhythmic effect, not a chord. You can also use a percussive "T" when blowing the chord—whichever sounds best to you. These are always on downbeat… understanding this will help your timing.

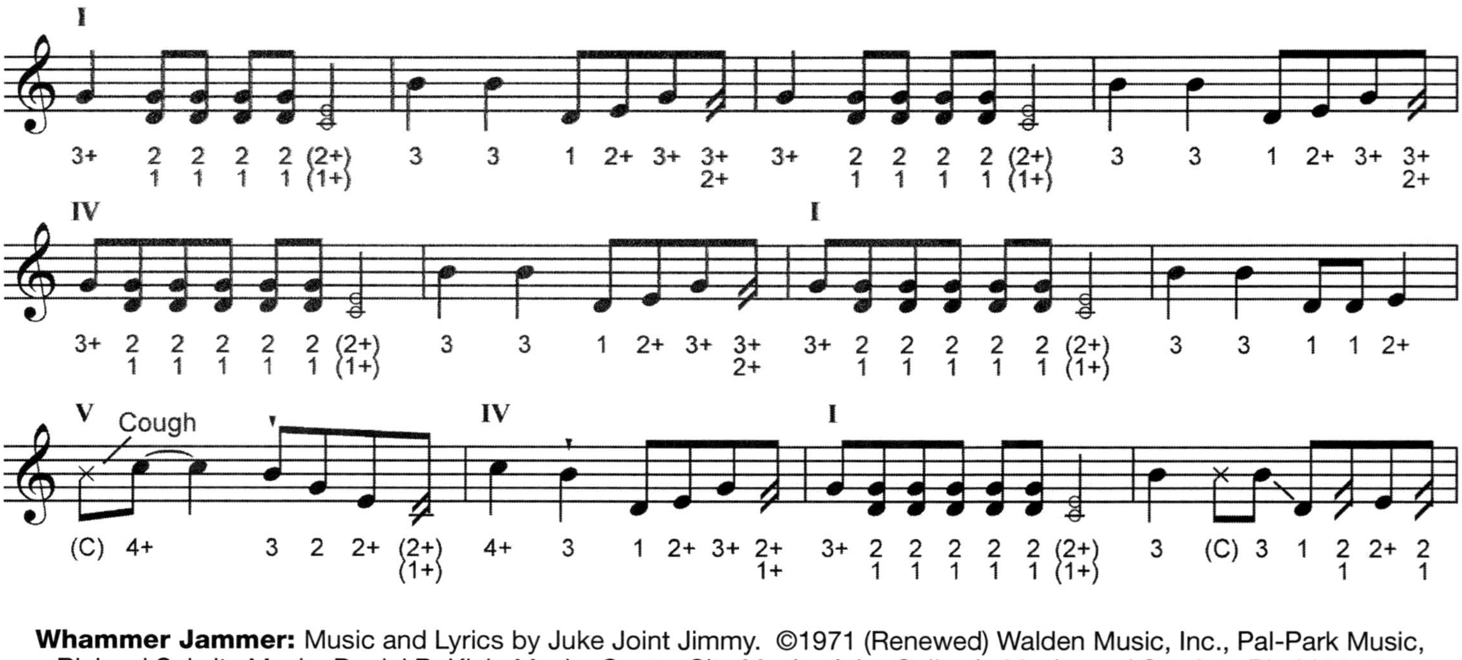

Whammer Jammer: Music and Lyrics by Juke Joint Jimmy. ©1971 (Renewed) Walden Music, Inc., Pal-Park Music, Richard Salwitz Music, Daniel B. Klein Music, Center City Music, John Geils, Jr. Music, and Stephen Bladd Music. All Rights Administered by Walden Music, Inc. This Arrangement © 2010 Walden Music, Inc., Pal-Park Music, Richard Salwitz Music, Daniel B. Klein Music, Center City Music, John Geils, Jr. Music, and Stephen Bladd Music. All Rights Reserved Including Public Performance. Used by Permission of Alfred Music Publishing, Co. Inc.

2nd Chorus – AAB Chorus Form (CD2, Track 16)

For these chords try "TA DL AH DL HU" or "TA KA TA KA HU." On the **V** Chord we start to see his use of the pull, which is a technique specific to tongue blocking (though it can be copied in a pucker on the lower three holes, it can only be done effectively on holes 4 and higher in the tongue block). This is where you block all of the holes in your embouchure with your tongue and pull off to sound the chord. If you would like to learn more about tongue blocking techniques, check out my book *Blues Harmonica Method Level 1, the Tongue Block Method* (MB21053BCD) in the *School of the Blues Lesson Series*.

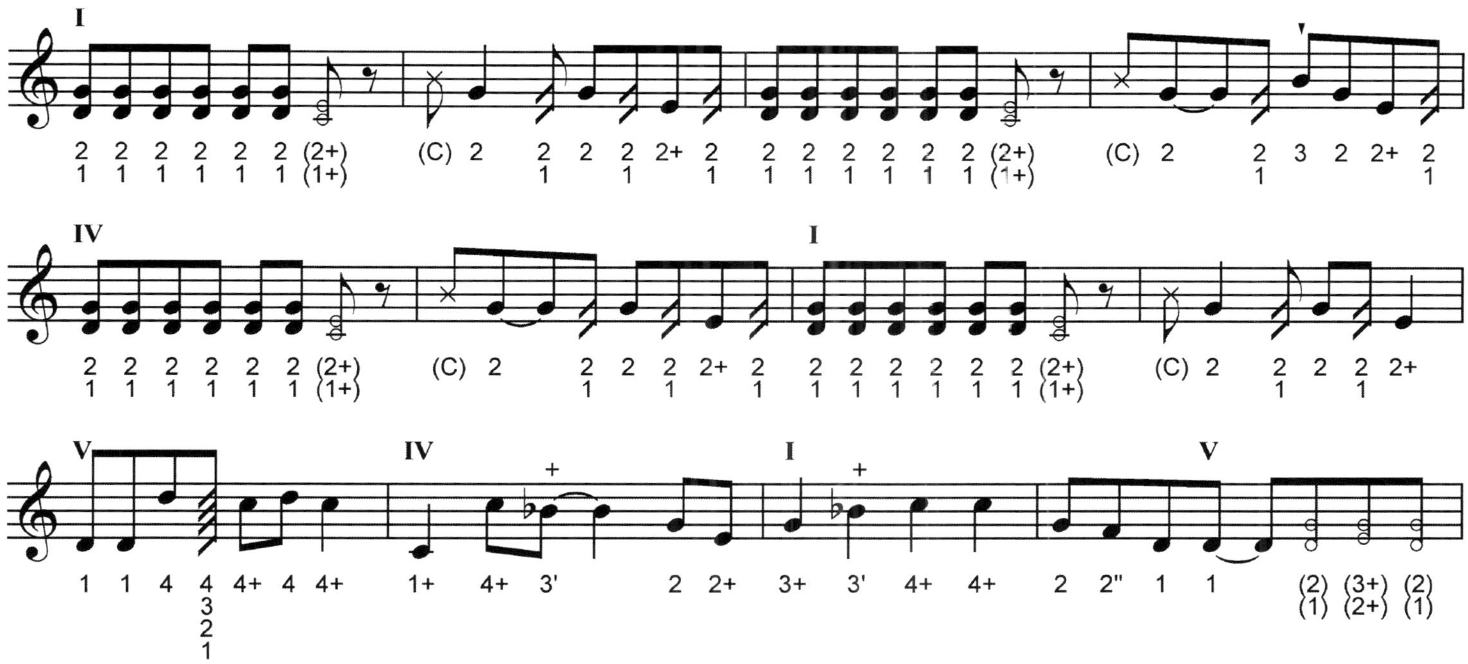

3rd Chorus – A B/A C Chorus Form (CD2, Track 17)

If you were puckering before, get your tongue out for some slaps and pulls… you have to tongue block for this chorus.

4th Chorus – A B/A C Chorus Form (CD2, Track 18)
Guitar enters here. Be sure to exhale before you start!

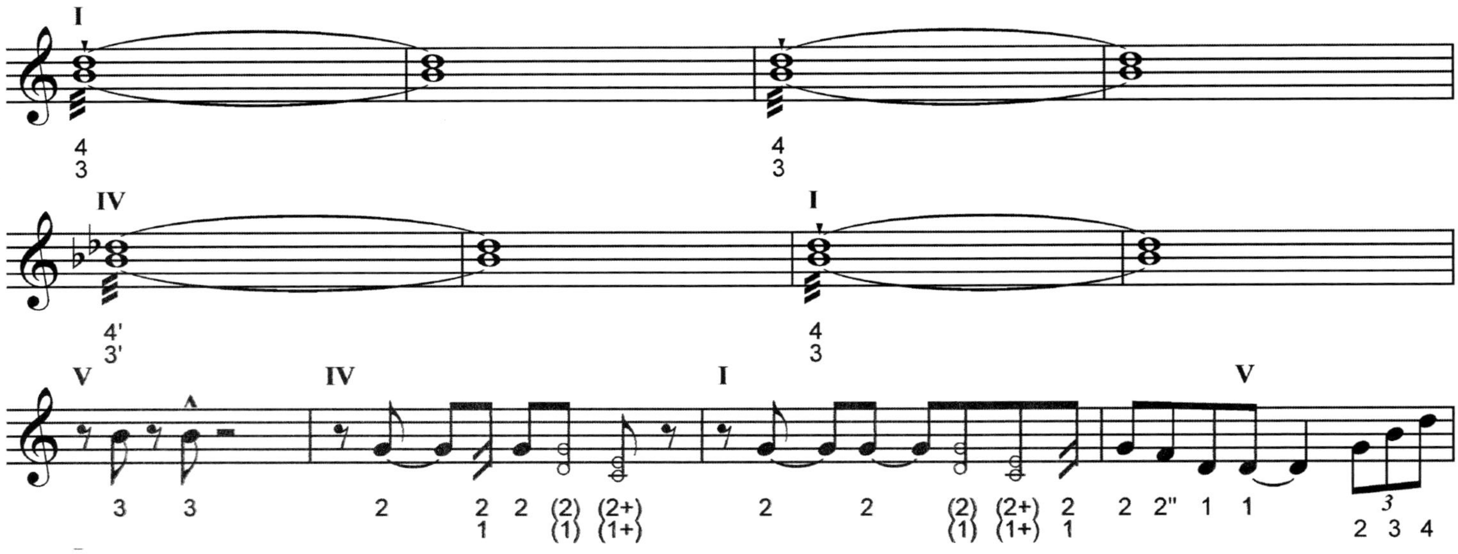

5th Chorus – A B/A C Chorus Form (CD2, Track 19)
Band comes in full-force here. Keep your embouchure relaxed and just slide up and down the harmonica for the triplets.

6th Break Chorus – ABC Chorus Form (CD2, Track 20)
We get our first of many breaks in this song. Dick starts with some shakes and follows up with dips on the 9+.

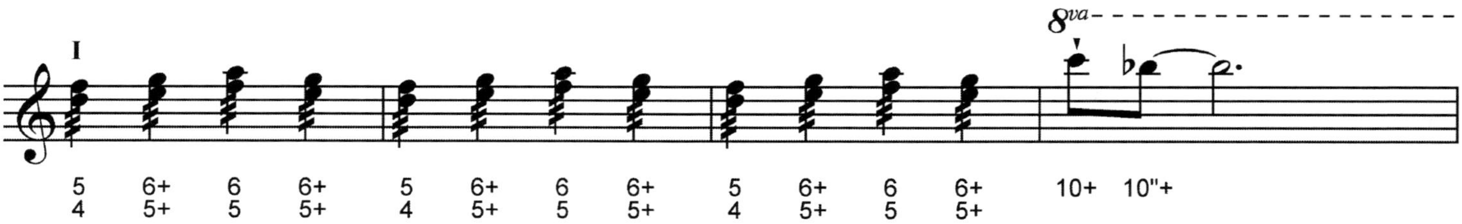

7th Break Chorus - ABC Chorus Form **(CD2, Track 21)**

8th Break Chorus – ABC Chorus Form **(CD2, Track 22)**

The first lick uses a pull, 4 bend, 4 draw. The release of the bend into the 4 draw should be articulated (not slurred). If you're puckering use "UH TA." If you're tongue blocking use "UH KA."

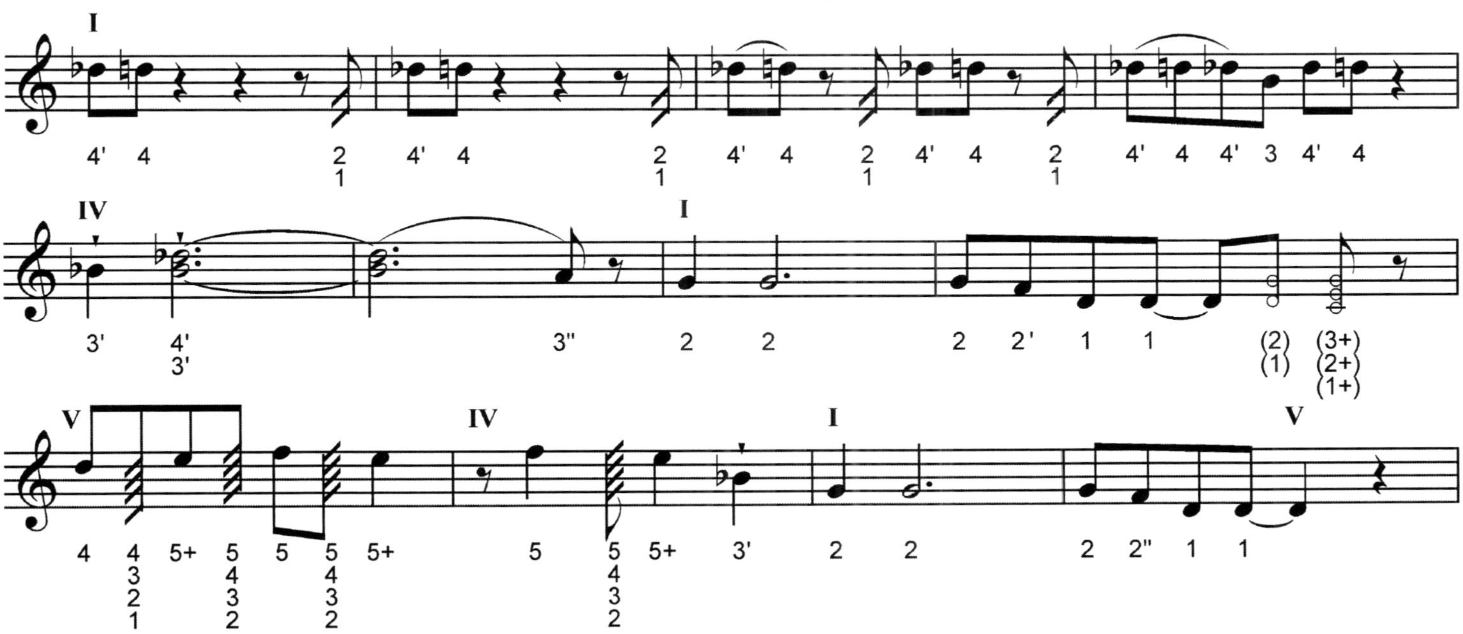

9th Break Chorus – ABC Chorus Form (CD2, Track 23)
On the V Chord he uses a Junior Wells-type lick (pucker here). As in the first chorus you'll want to experiment with what works for you. I use "UH DL AH" for each triplet.

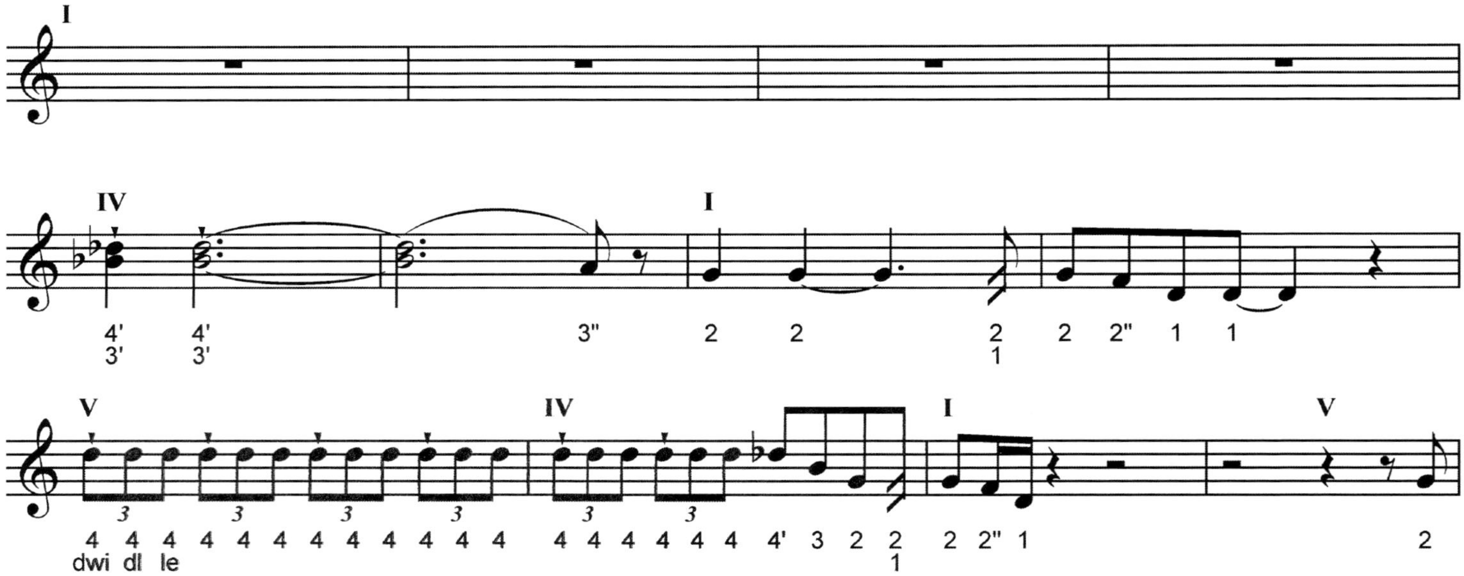

10th Chorus – A B/A C Chorus Form (CD2, Track 24)
Finally our last chorus—and it's smokin' fast!

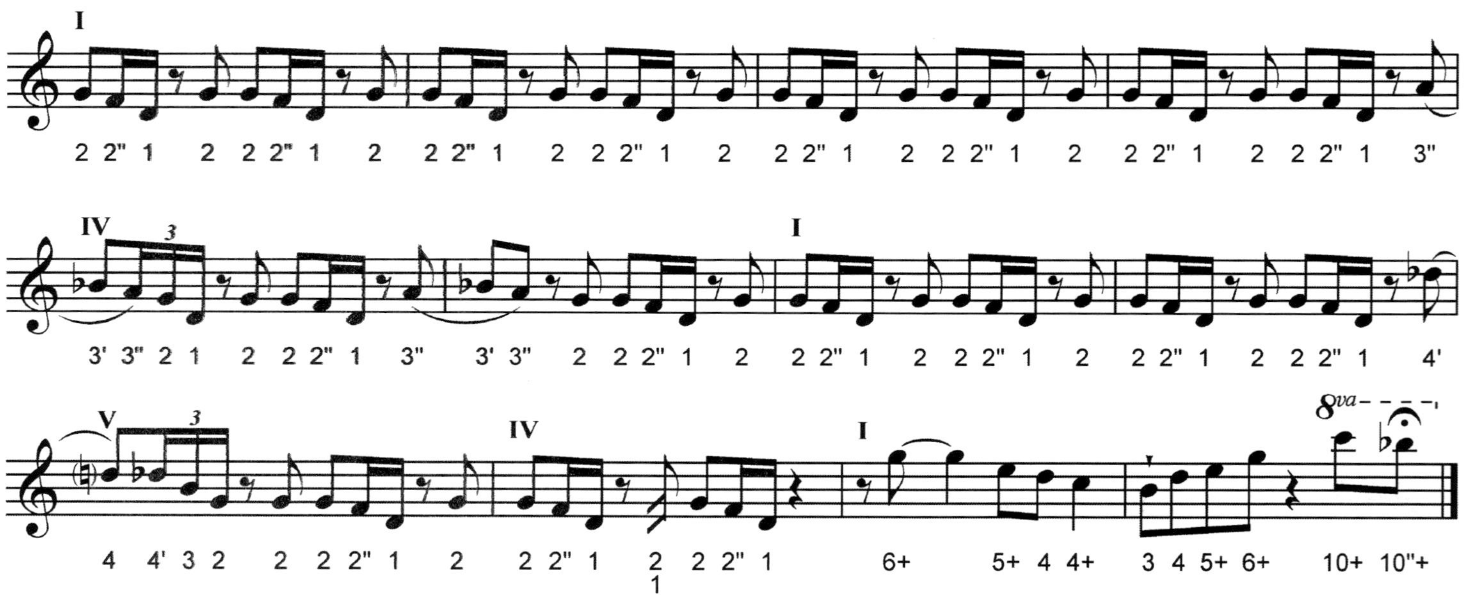

What to Say To The Band
Song: Whammer Jammer **(CD2, Track 25 Full Song / CD2, Track 26 20% Slow)**
Key: A
Groove: Shuffle
Other: Watch me for breaks

Notes: This song could be done without rehearsal (at a jam session), but every time I've heard a student try to do it with a pickup band it was messy. The band really needs to pay attention and the harp player needs to be very good and obvious about their signals. For this reason I would recommend you play this with a band you've rehearsed the song with.

Some players are self conscious about performing the scream in the 9th Chorus. In my recorded version I gave you an option for this. In this case I play a 6 draw with a little 7 draw bleeding in to make it sound mean. The 6 draw is follow by 6' 5 4. Experiment with ideas of your own and find what works for you!

Play-Along Track (CD2, Track 27 Play-Along Track, Starting on Chorus 4)
There are two elements to this song that make it pretty much impossible to make a jam track for.

1) The opening uses hits that free-float in time
2) The first three choruses are played without the band

This is fine in a live setting where you can signal the band when to perform hits and when to come in after the opening three choruses, but it doesn't work for a jam track where you and the track can't communicate. So... the jam track I have provided for you starts on the fourth chorus where the band comes in. Practice the opening three choruses on your own with a metronome.

Whammer Jammer

By: Magic Dick

Key: E (A Harmonica in 2nd Position) / Groove: Shuffle

Transcribed by David Barrett

Whammer Jammer

Music and Lyrics by Juke Joint Jimmy. ©1971 (Renewed) Walden Music, Inc., Pal-Park Music, Richard Salwitz Music, Daniel B. Klein Music, Center City Music, John Geils, Jr. Music, and Stephen Bladd Music.
All Rights Administered by Walden Music, Inc. This Arrangement © 2010 Walden Music, Inc., Pal-Park Music, Richard Salwitz Music, Daniel B. Klein Music, Center City Music, John Geils, Jr. Music, and Stephen Bladd Music.
All Rights Reserved Including Public Performance. Used by Permission of Alfred Music Publishing, Co. Inc.

I 0:36 - 3rd Chorus
I 0:50 - 4th Chorus
I 1:04 - 5th Chorus

1:18 - 6th Chorus
1:32 - 7th Chorus
1:46 - 8th Chorus

2:00 - 9th Chorus (Ah!!!)
dwi dl le
2:14 - 10th Chorus

Chapter 10 – "Butter Strut" Song Study

In my opinion, Paul Butterfield, though very much a blues man, was the greatest Rock harmonica player to ever live. His bluesy phrases, powerful lines and willingness to experiment with new ideas made him a huge influence on everyone that followed him—especially the more rockin' players I've mentioned. Though this song doesn't bear much resemblance to his playing, it uses his ideas, the blues scale (which he used most of the time), movement and approach to the powerful sound the harmonica has to offer.

The head of our song uses basically three chords, the **I**, **IV** and **V**. I say basically because there are passing chords and the main chords do have some treatments to them—but for our soloing focus, thinking of the basic chords will do just fine. The voicing used by the guitar for most of the chords in this song are Root-5th. With the lack of the 3rd of the chord to tell us whether to play in major or minor, we have our choice of which way to go, but this type of voicing almost always leans towards a minor, more dark feel. For this reason the blues scale is a great choice for your selection of notes. Below are the basic chords we're using. I show the major-3rd of the chord in the arpeggio, though you'll most likely want to ignore its use. We'll call this the **A Section**.

Ex. 10.1 – A Section

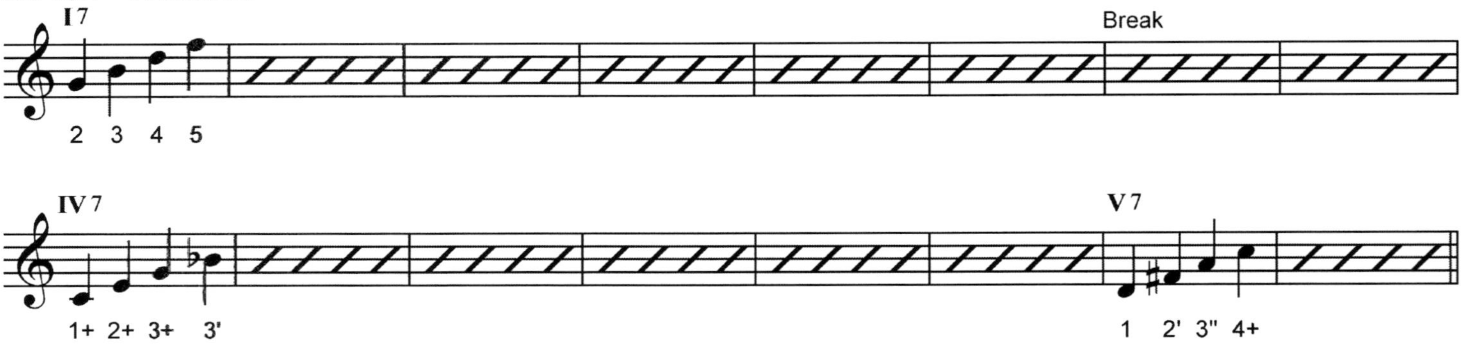

The A Section is played twice and then goes to what we'll call a bridge. The ***Bridge*** is a deviation in form (commonly both in length and chords used). We'll call this the **B Section**.

Ex. 10.2 – B Section

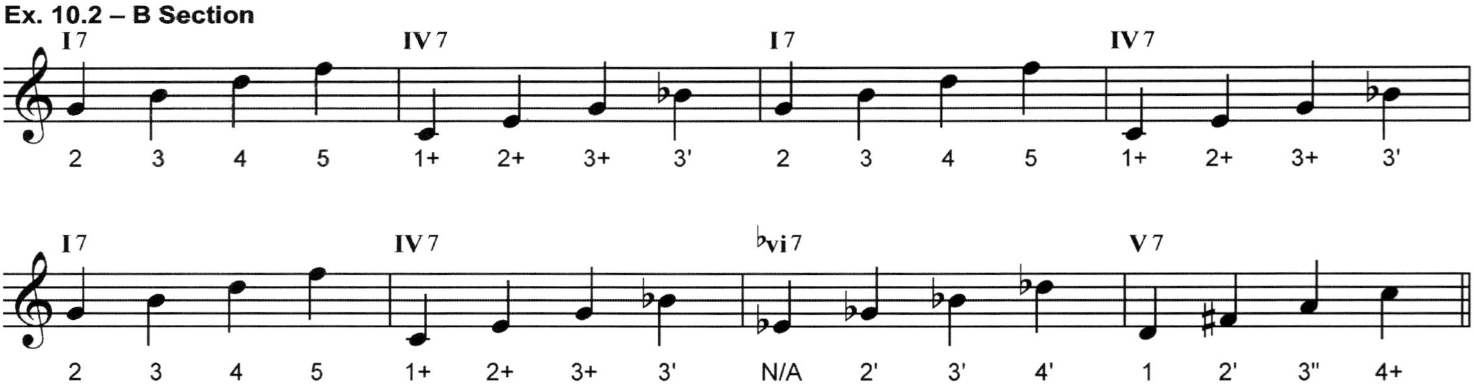

The A Section returns and then the solo starts. We're essentially playing a modal blues (no chord change) for the solo. The blues scale is a perfect choice for this solo section—and that's what I use. There IS a second chord present—the **flat-VII** Chord, which we can ignore or use if you want to be more melodic; the notes are **F—A—C**. These notes are easily found on the harmonica and it makes sense to use these now and again to tip your hat to the chord change (gives the impression that we know what we're doing!). Since this is where you'll let loose the most during this song, it's a good idea to loop this section and spend a lot of time experimenting with note combination based from the chords; sections of the blues scale; licks that you've learned in this book; and of course licks from your vocabulary.

Ex. 10.3 – Solo Section

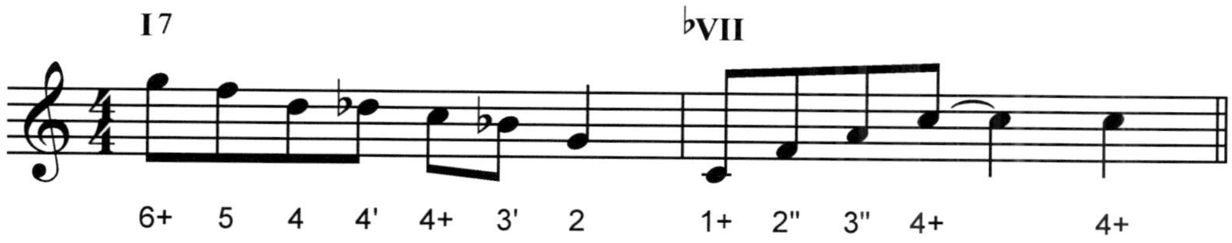

At the end of the solo section the **flat-VI** and **V** Chords return (same as the last two measures of the bridge) to bring in the first eight measures of the A Section as a way to bring a piece of the head back and make for a nice transition to the guitar solo. Including these two measures the solo section is 24 measures in length. While John Garcia solos you can either sit out until the head returns at the end or play notes that match the two chords to keep the texture of the harmonica in the mix.

The A Section returns at the end of the song to bring it to a close. The tag (last two measures of the section) is played three times at the end—this is a common tool to use for the ending of a song.

What to Say To The Band

Song: Butter Strut **(CD2, Track 28 Full Song / CD2, Track 29 20% Slow)**
Key: G
Groove: Rock Beat
Other: Watch me for breaks

Notes: This song in no way represents something other musicians would be familiar with—in other words, it doesn't use the chord progression of a previously recorded famous song and no one should be expected to know. For this reason, this song can only be played with a band that has studied the song and has rehearsed it.

Play-Along Track **(CD2, Track 30 Play-Along Track with Guitar Solo / CD2, Track 31 Play-Along Track without Guitar Solo)**

The provided jam track is in its full form. Have fun!

Butter Strut

Tribute to Paul Butterfield By David Barrett

Key: G (C Harmonica in 2nd Position) / Start: From the I (One Chord)

Butter Strut - Page 1

I7 3rd Chorus (B Section) - 1:08
I7 4th Chorus (A Section) - 1:25
Harmonica Solo - 2:00 (Time will float for dramatic effect)
Cup opens as note is held

I 7
♭VII
I 7 A Section Returns for 6 Measures - 2:51
Guitar Solo - 3:04
25
I 7 A Section - 3:58

5 5 4 (6) 5 4 (6) (6) 4 (6) 4 (6) 4' 3 2 (4') 4+ (4') 4+ (4') 2 2 2" 1
5 5 5 5 5 3' 3' 3'
IV 7
1+ 4+ 4+ 2 (4') 4+ 4' 4 5 4 5 4 4+ 4 (4') 2 2" 1 4+ 4+ 2 (4') 4+ 4' 4 5 6+ 6+ 4' 4 5 4 5 4 5 6+
3' 3' 1+ 1+ 3'
V 7
4+ 4+ 2 (4') 4+ 4+ (4') 2 (4') 2' 2' 1 2' 2' 1 2' 2' 1 2'
3' 3' 3'
2' 2' 1 2' 2' 1 2' 2' 1 2' 2' 2' 1 2' 2' 1 2' 2' 1 2'
4 (6) 4' 3 2 (4') 4+ 4 6+
5 3' 3+

Chapter 11 – How to be a Great Rock Harmonica Player

By Jason Ricci

Rock and Roll is the broadest, most inclusive of musical categories or genres—so familiarity with a broad range of styles provides simple, necessary components which are essential in the playing, homework, listening and overall development of a great Rock harmonica player. I am presently a "Blues artist" for almost all purposes (though I usually call my music Rock and Roll—and actually I prefer just the term "Music"). I'm on a Blues label and working in Blues venues... being marketed to Blues fans. When this Blues label asked me, "What category of music do you want your albums to be placed under in the stores," I chose Rock. Why? Well, first there is a bit of industry explanation needed. In brief, an artist signing with a label can only pick one category. The bigger stores, and most of the little or independent ones, will never file you differently on their racks after you've debuted a national album in a certain genre of music, i.e. Rock, Country, Blues, Rap, World, etc. This may seem like unnecessary industry crap from a bitter musician, but it's metaphorical of a mindset that we ourselves create as artists when we classify ourselves with titles, genres, eras, styles etc... I want to be free to explore.

My music heroes, independent of genre are: Miles, Paganini, Little Walter, Janis Joplin, Sun Ra, Lou Reed, Tom Waits, Bjork, The Misfits, Danzig and Bob Dylan. These artists were always changing, always growing and always exploring. Rock too has always been in change—in form and names, and in major or minute sub category classifications. You have Rock and Roll, Punk Rock, Garage Rock, Classic Rock, 50s, 60s, 70s, 80s, etc. Rock, Blues Rock, Metal, Speed Metal, Death Metal, Black Metal, Alternative Rock, Grunge Rock, Hair Metal, Rockabilly, Country Rock, Rock Steady, Hip Hop Rock, Trance Rock, and on and on.... and why the hell not? Silly isn't it, though? The further you go with the overtly specific and idiosyncratic minute definitions, the more you focus in and away from the actual art and feeling of the music... and miss the forest for its trees... and the more you prove what Muddy Waters said a long time ago, "There's only two kinds of music, good music and bad music."

I'm an individual that accepts, because of a commitment to growth, that I don't, and hopefully can't, know for sure what I will be playing or listening to, or even where I might want to live, what I might want to wear or anything else. This doesn't mean I live a reckless life, full of constant chaos (well maybe a bit). It does mean I don't like setting limits, building fences, or making rules or definitions to describe my own personal artistic future—as a player, singer, songwriter, performer, writer, person or musician. I know for sure that life is changing all around me. And as Dylan said in "The Times They Are A-Changin'," "you'd better start swimming or you'll sink like a stone." I want to believe/hope that I will be a different person five years from now. I have enough rigorous rules, laws, bills, titles and other limitations set in place by society and our government, as well as others in my everyday life. While Rock has a reckless reputation (we like it), the genre is packed full of stellar, disciplined, well-versed artists. These players have often studied formally at the best music schools in the world as well as at the feet of obscure or famous artists, blues or otherwise. These same Rock bands can and do occupy headlining spots at BLUES FESTIVALS. They are hated by the purists, but loved by the masses. They produce fans and ticket buyers, give clout to the festivals themselves, and bring newcomers to Blues Music Festivals. Sometimes they are great players as well.

Rarely these days do people say they're going to see a "Rock show" or a "Rock band." They say they're going to see "The Black Crowes," or "Phish." (Funny that no one says "HEAR.") Yet you frequently hear fans say they're going to see a "Blues band," a "Jazz band" or a "Bluegrass band," as if the artist playing is secondary to the style of music! Great artists are reduced, or respectively and honorably reduced/awarded/emasculated to a simple style of music and the vague impressions that leaves on the mind. Something as seemingly innocent, yet passionately debated, as genre classification, can make or break someone's career, financial future and fan base; and thus the quality of their artistic and personal life. The great multi-genre, multi-instrumentalist Clarence "Gate Mouth" Brown passionately and frequently refused to ever answer to, be named as, or confide within any title of Blues, Country, Rock, Jazz or whatever. His music reflected this. He was far from a "jack of all trades and master of none." Gate Mouth was a great and accomplished multi-styled, open-minded player who will always be remembered by his fans as himself, both a human being and an artist, no matter what instrument he was on, what clothes he wore, what color he was, where he came from or what style of music most closely resembled what he was playing!

But since we have to pick a style to communicate with fans, clubs, audiences and stores... Rock intrigues me the most. The non-specific, all-encompassing variety of artists that fall under this heading by default means that, more so than others genres of music, Rock gives the artist a unique identity beyond just parameters, perceptions and boundaries. In short, if you want to be a Rock musician you need an identity of your own, your own spin, your own name and your own style. This is a lot. It's intimidating and a tough musical path technically, spiritually and emotionally. Many players and people are perfectly content within the well accepted, comfortable and proven traditions of artists that have crafted their careers by sounding like other artists before them. We know the greats sounded good—that's why they're the greats. Do I sound any good as me? The greats sounded good as themselves—maybe you will too? I do... and I have company.

Genres

Genres indicate mostly musical texture, volume, instrumentation and chords; lyrical and musical subject matter; and melodies. When I revisit Rock and Roll bands of the 60s and 70s especially, and listen to those albums in their entirety, I'm hearing Blues, Country, Jazz, Folk, Eastern and so many other styles of music. From song to song styles change: within one album, within one tune or epic jam or, by some of the greats within one single lick. Think about Janis Joplin or more specifically Janis with Big Brother and the Holding Company. Think Jimi Hendrix, The Byrds, Canned Heat, The Butterfield Blues Band and WAR!. All of those groups, and many others, had ingredients of Funk, Rock, Latin, Country, Eastern, Folk and Classical. So we now have an idea of this Rock player's mind set, philosophy, and belief system (or lack thereof).

How to be a Great Rock Harmonica Player

Harmonica is an instrument that is rarely played well, technically, by Rock players. Not so strangely, without naming names, many popular harmonica players have really not been very good harmonica players. Rock music still sells more records than any other style of music (Rap Included). The harmonica as an instrument was, and still is for those alive and kickin', a secondary instrument. It takes a back seat to their voice, guitar, lyrics, etc. In the stadium setting the harmonica frequently is a novelty instrument—an oddly shaped tambourine substitute, a whistle, or curious, but short, distraction in the show. Players like Alan Wilson, Paul Butterfield, Pig Pen, Norton Buffalo, John Popper, Howard Levy, Magic Dick, Jimmy Z, Steven Tyler, Mick Jagger and others have succeeded in exposing literally millions of people to the merits of this instrument's abilities, on platinum and gold recordings and to stadiums full of future Little-Walter-album-buying harmonica fans. Yet still some short-sighted elitists value their knowledge of the obscure more than the music of their favorite performers. They like being the few and rare in the know. From their ivory towers and history books, rare 45s and audiophile tube stereos they argue the true musicianship of some of these names. These same moldy figs argue in their genre-specific magazines (that don't sell well) the same subject matter, with added genre qualifications about artists that work within the confines, venues, labels and agencies of their beloved traditional music forms. They just like to sound important—for them it's fun.

When I was starting to get gigs I actually really needed the money to live on. I had chosen to make my living as a harmonica player, hopefully a Blues harmonica player that wouldn't have to sing. However, as I fell deeper and deeper into the poverty level I began to—quite literally—change my tune. I had students wanting to learn John Popper licks and Charlie McCoy licks. I had gigs where I had to sing back-up vocals on Jethro Tull songs. I had gigs where I had to sing all night by myself (how I learned... and am still learning... and now finally liking!). I had to play sax solos from Bob Seger songs, learn horn parts from Tower of Power tunes, play keyboard parts and other instruments just to contribute and get paid. This is normal for musicians. Harmonica players don't like to do this, and they blame others for their lack of gigs instead of helping themselves, making a few bucks—by learning a new lick, trick or song. I've even had to frequently create ideas using knowledge of root note harmony and rhythm to work with artists' original music that were not written for, nor intended to house, harmonica. Well, I got paid and it even helped my Blues playing. This is what makes me and other Rock players great. In doing these things (that I hated at that time), I learned note combinations, licks, scales and "rules" of other styles of music.

For the sake of time I will attempt to simplify the potential Rock harp student's initial study to a trinity of three basic American styles of music. One is Blues, the mother of Rock and Roll, where the harmonica is often at the fore front of the band or is the central instrument; and the home of the most accomplished, prolific and imitated harmonica players. Two is Country, a music form that developed simultaneously and parallel with Blues and Rock. Three is, arrogantly enough, Rock itself. An overview of these three styles should prepare the Rock harmonica student with a good start and some great tools to deal with the broad range of texture, chords and rhythms that a Rock band could throw at an unsuspecting harp player. Please keep in mind that these are very simplistic overviews of styles of music that any artist could study for their whole lives without learning everything. Entire books, DVD's, classes and seminars exist for the study of each of these musical genres, even for the harmonica. Additionally, as a harp footnote: I will be covering these styles with our most common second position (also known as cross harp) in mind for now. Of course all positions should be considered in further study.

Country

This is a style of music that, like others, encompasses some musical generalities, stereotypes and preconceived structures. Accents are frequently on beats 1 and 3 and the "up-beats" of the music. The scales are usually very major (except of course in a strictly minor tune). The Mixolydian mode (major scale with a flat-7th) is a common treatment for most major or major-ish country tunes. Using that flat-7th sparingly, or over chords where the flat-7th is present (A7 for example), can add a Bluegrass or Blues flavor to your country playing. Be careful if you're coming from a Blues background. The flat-7th could be a hair too familiar to your muscle memory and lick patterns, both conscious and subconscious. Use of this flat-7th should be reserved for adding spice, not as a main ingredient. Try some other notes in its place (such as the major 6th) for a bit til you're sure you're playing it when it's called for—or when YOU want it there (for the Bluesy quality it offers).

Learning to avoid the flat-7th altogether in favor of a major-7th or major-6th makes for a more refined, harmonically aware and well-versed country/major key harmonica player. A great musician knows where the main notes of any style are and when to accentuate them or break the rules by ignoring them and focusing on others. Popular country scale tones, other than the root of course, are the 2nd, 3rd, 6th and 7th. Playing a simple country lick like 4, 4, 3" and 2 give's you an idea of the happy, soulful country tones needed on a tune like "Don't Roll Those Blood Shot Eyes At Me." While I'm at it, Jimmy Reed and Slim Harpo rock these country-tinged licks in some of the most popular BLUES tunes of all time.

For minor country tunes, scales like Harmonic Minor and Natural Minor tend to feel more harmonically appropriate then the simple Pentatonic or Blues scales. The more you study all these styles of music the more you see how they influence each other, steal from each other and ultimately rule each other out. They have much more in common than they do in difference—like us as people. Listen to Kirk "Jelly Roll" Johnson, Charlie McCoy, TJ Klay, PT Gazelle, Terry McMillan and Buddy Greene, as well as the guitar, banjo, fiddle, and piano players they play with. Country rocks!

Blues

I cannot overstate the importance of an in-depth study and absorption of this music. When I took my first harmonica lesson (I was 15 years old) my teacher said, "If you want to be a good harp player you're going to have to listen to Blues." My heart sank. I later fell in love with not only Blues harmonica players but also the music itself. I stated earlier that Blues is the mother of Rock and Roll—where the harmonica is often at the forefront of the band and is the central instrument, and the home of the most accomplished, prolific and imitated harmonica players. Blues has a lot of fire and a lot of earth elements in it. It's a very primal musical form with its subject matter being frequently about women, men, whisky, sex, drugs, loss, spiritual confusion, human joys and earthly pleasures. Not unlike the familiar mantra Sex, Drugs and Rock and Roll. Rock and Roll has had its demonic and satanic myths, legends and exploits and Blues has had its own as well. These two forms are tied deeply to each other—folklore, history, songs, artists and basic musical structure. Let's explore more.

When breaking down the 12-Bar Blues structure we meet with the **I IV V** chord change. This chord change and its variations can be found throughout Rock music, and also in most other forms of American music like Jazz and Country. It's a default canvas to paint from and the list of Jazz, Country and Rock tunes that contain this form could fill this entire book, probably hundreds of times. Rock and Roll's first big stars and big hit songs were simply Blues songs using a **I IV V** chord change, sung by white musicians on TV and the radio with a bit more of a country twang. From Elvis and Buddy Holly to the Beatles and The Stones and right up to today's acts like the Black Crowes and even Marilyn Manson, we see this familiar chord progression reappear again and again. Learning the root notes of the **I IV V**, their basic harmonic extensions and the familiar phrasings, licks, and clichés used in blues will make you the most solid, intuitive and ready Rock player you can be. The Blues Scale and the Minor Pentatonic Scale (same as the blues scale without the flat-5) are the basis of most the licks we have in this music genre. The key notes within these scales are the flat-3 (3', 6OB and 10"+) and the Flat-5 (1', 4' and 7OD). Incidentally, the flat-5 was called by the classical musical community, or at that time THE music community, "The Devil's Interval." This was a religiously based term and religiously enforced law that prohibited its use at one time (circa 1700). So, needless to say, as Rock players we like our Devil's interval a lot. Use it, Rockers!

Other elements of Blues commonly found in the Rock environment, and needed by any instrumentalist, are an awareness of space, leaving space, solo structure, call and response, repetition, simplicity of form and an attention to groove and feel more than technical structure. Never forget though that Rock breaks all the rules by definition and all these principles are to be studied, learned, followed, but ultimately discarded or not (or in partiality) for the ultimate individuality of the artist over the musical form. THE BOTTOM LINE IS ROCK AND ROLL IS ABOUT FUN and is all about you and your musical WILL.

Rock and Roll

I still refuse to confine Rock and Roll to a series of categories, labels, structures and rules, and that really is the ultimate thesis of this work. It really can't be done and certainly cannot be done within the confines of this article's space. However, certain constants do remain. The characteristics of Blues, Country, Classical, Jazz, Eastern, Psychedelic, Hip Hop, Metal, etc., all permeate through its various forms and more importantly its artists. So in short, a constant or control, a postulate in Rock in Roll is that anything goes and it's free to be all-inclusive. Here are some generalities associated with Rock and Roll. Generalities are of course based on the general, the general is of course the usual and the usual is not true all the time, hence the following stereotypes are just that.

1) Rock music has a lot of fast licks and fancy playing.
2) Rock Music is frequently loud and has affected tones and electronic effects, and makes use of modern technology and innovations in the areas of both gear and musicality.
3) Rock Music contains a lot of darker, more bluesy, dissonant and riskier musical textures than most forms of music.

The list could go on, but let's start with these, and address the first stereotype: fast licks and fancy playing. There are certain patterns—blow, blow, draw, draw, and lots of others—that can be learned and implemented by even a novice on the harmonica. These particular patterns can be played very fast and very easily to the delight of audiences everywhere. They are parlor tricks in a way, and every instrument has them. They are simply licks that are easy to play fast, sound mostly good, and are impressive to the uninitiated. I am by no means dismissing these licks, as I believe everything has its place and showmanship is a big part of all music. I say learn them, study them and use them sparingly. The name John Popper probably comes to the learned reader's mind here. This man is in no way at all a perpetrator of the simple breathing patterns at high speeds I'm talking about here. Yes he does them indeed, but he's a creative genius, working mostly out of the Mixolydian mode in cross harp to great melodic effect. He's the Eddie Van Halen of the instrument and THE player the harmonica community needed most in the Rock and Roll spotlight, whether they realized it or not. By playing super-fast, flute or guitar-like licks at mesmerizing speeds, he really has taken the instrument, for many fans, out of the folky, rack-mounted, breathy, chordy novelty instrument zone and into the forefront of technicality and legitimacy as a real Rockin' instrument. Magic Dick and the other artists I listed earlier have done their parts for decades and have helped vindicate our instrument out of the "toy" arena, but Popper really hit the public hard. Sugar Blue most certainly deserves mention here, and is only over-shadowed by Popper when counting record sales and influence on the greater public. Popper is far from the first guy to play fast, and many before and after him have done so with more varied use of scales, harmony, modes, positions and rhythm—but this does not downplay Popper's contribution as a platinum-selling harp blower, singer and songwriter.

Rock harmonica players that have used speed while maintaining what we'll call "Harmonic Integrity" (attention to major, minor, chord structure, melody, etc.) include:

1) Pat Ramsey
2) Norton Buffalo
3) Mark Ford
4) Howard Levy
5) Peter Mad Cat Ruth
6) Jason Ricci (I would be implementing false humility not to include myself here. I'm comfortable doing so in spite of the arrogance a reader might interpret and would argue that my inclusion is for the intent of the reader's knowledge. Besides, Rock and Roll is an attitude and Rock and Rollers have attitudes!)

It's my opinion that Pat Ramsey is to Rock harmonica what Little Walter was to the Blues harp. He played fast in a controlled and deliberate fashion, using mostly the Pentatonic Scale, Blues Scale, Major Scale and Mixolydian Scale. His phrasing echoes the great Rock guitarists of the 60s and 70s like Eric Clapton, Johnny Winter, Rick Derringer and Mike Bloomfield; and even more modern players like Walter Trout, Stevie Ray Vaughn and Robben Ford. He stayed focused on blue notes, giving his fast chops more "balls." His amplified sound was much like a guitar and sounded this way even when, in his 20s, he recorded on Johnny Winter's record "White Hot and Blue." Pat's recordings can be purchased on the internet. There are three—soon to be four—solo albums, the Johnny Winter album and various sideman sessions. I have numerous videos explaining elements of Pat's playing on YouTube, but the student of Rock harmonica or Blues should explore him on their own with great curiosity. Pat Ramsey is one of the very few players who have ever achieved greatness on this instrument without studying intently the work of Little Walter. His take on the instrument is as unique as Walter's himself, Paul Butterfield's, Howard Levy's or Paul DeLay's. Pat's playing also depicts the last two Rock postulates outlined above. Let's return to those.

The second item I listed above is, "Rock music is frequently loud, has affected tones and electronic effects, and makes use of modern technology and innovations in the areas of both gear and musicality." This is true, again as a stereotype. If you want to play Rock music you'll need a big amp, or devices that make it possible for you to play pretty loud, and it helps to have some effects to add flavor—to sound like different instruments, for example. Most of the other instruments on the bandstand use them as well these days, even the drums (if there is a real drummer). Why should you limit your range? Plus, you might like it! Effects make you play and hear differently. This is akin to altered states or drug-taking, which I will not comment on here other than to say it has had its influence on all music forms.

My third item is, "Rock music contains more dark, bluesy, dissonant and risky musical textures than most forms of music." There are many happy Rock songs, however the music has to "rock" and darkness rocks harder than light in the Rock world. A great Rock player puts a little evil in the music every time. The use of Blues and "blue notes," and the lyrical and instrumental grounding of Rock in Blues, makes for a great Dark Rock God! Consider this: Black Sabbath started as a Blues band; and Prince of Darkness Ozzy Osborne started out as a harmonica player! (See "the Wizard" as well as other early tunes and video footage). You will need, as a great Rock player, to know your Blues history well.

You might not have to sell your soul to the devil, but it will help to sell your solo.

In conclusion... Have fun. Study everything. Keep an open mind. Listen to other instruments. Find where people are not right or wrong. Play fast and loud—with technique or without it—but use some taste if you want to impact the largest audience of both listeners and players. Wear funky clothes. Get lots of tattoos if you want. Do your hair crazy. Get some earrings. Use effects pedals, big amps and gizmos. Know your history, but keep your left eye on the future. Have sympathy for the devil and Rock on!

Chapter 12 – **Recommended Artists**

Here are some artists for you to check out. Keep in mind that the best players of today were avid imitators of the great players of our past. Half of your practice time should be spent studying other harmonica player's ideas.

- Mark Ford
- Andy Just
- John Mayall
- Magic Dick (J Geils Band)
- Paul Butterfield
- Lee Oskar (WAR)
- Darrel Mansfield
- Pat Ramsey
- Jason Ricci
- Kim Wilson
- John Popper
- Huey Lewis
- John Sebastian (Doors)
- Bob Dylan (Folk-Rock)
- Neil Young (Folk Rock)
- Norton Buffalo (Steve Miller)
- Fingers Taylor (Jimmy Buffett)
- Steve Baker

I asked my good friend and respected educator/artist Steve Baker for any recommended additions and he added the names below. I also asked Steve to tell us a little bit more about his history—he's one of the best well-rounded musicians on harp that I know.

- Mark Breitfelder
- Mark Feltham (Nine Below Zero, Godley & Creme, Oasis and many more)
- Jim Fitting (Played with The The)
- Jimmy Z (The Eurythmics, "Missionary Man" is one of the best exposed titles featuring rock harp)
- Peter Hope Evans (Pete Townsend)
- Hyper Harp
- Steven Tyler (Aerosmith)
- Bruce Springsteen
- Peter "Madcat" Ruth (was already playing rock harp in the late 60s with Sky King)

Steve writes, "I played in rock bands for many years in the 1980s. I first started playing what could be termed 'rock harp' with Tony Sheridan in 1979. Tony had the Beatles as his backing band before they became famous and his music was old school rock'n'roll and R&B so I learned to accompany loads of stuff by Ray Charles, Elvis, Little Richard, Jerry Lee Lewis and others as well as taking my first steps to playing ballads ("Will You Still Love Me Tomorrow" for example). When I began playing non-blues material in a rock band in 1981, my jumping off point was Magic Dick and Feltham, as they were already there (Dick was a major inspiration for Feltham).

Both were/are basically blues stylists who adapted this approach to the music their bands were playing and I was hearing other possibilities. I soon began incorporating elements from sax players (horn riffs), from whom I also acquired my approach to playing funky. I also borrowed many ideas about how to construct rock riffs from Keith Richards and other rock guitarists, and many melodic ideas from Jerry Garcia and Dicky Betts. This wasn't a conscious process but I had absorbed the ideas through hearing their music and only recognized where I had got them from in retrospect. They fitted the music we were playing so I used them.

I found that another really cool way to use the harp as an accompanying instrument was to lay down 'sound carpets' which moved with the chord changes, rather like a keyboard player. Of course the harmonic possibilities of this are limited but it's surprising what you can do. So in a nutshell, as well as playing blues-based stuff I also incorporated elements borrowed from horn players, guitarists and keyboards."

Chapter 13 – Notation Key

Technique	Example	Description	Reference
Blow & Draw	 3 4 5+	When a hole number stands by itself (3) the hole is to be inhaled (draw). When a hole number is followed by a plus (5+) the hole is to be exhaled (blow).	All Books
Bend Slash(es) next to hole number	 2 2" 1 1	For each degree of a bend on the harmonica a small slash will be used following the hole number. The 3 draw half step bend (B-flat) is notated with one slash (3'). The 3 draw whole step bend (A) is notated with two slashes (3"). The 3 draw minor third bend (A-flat) is notated with three slashes (3'").	C1 p60-68 BHTDVD12 S1
Slur Curved line above or below connecting two note heads of different pitch	 6' 6 6	The slur indicates to slide (or in our case bend) smoothly from the pitch of one note to the pitch of another note. This symbol is also used for the **Tie**. The tie connects to notes of the SAME PITCH and directs you to combine the duration of the two notes.	General Notation
Dip Small "V" shape above a note	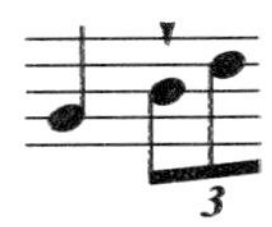 2 3 4	Note starts bent (around a quartertone or half step) and releases quickly. Some players use the articulations: Ya, Gya, Dya, Dwa, Tya or Kya. A dip is a more concise way to notate this technique compared to writing out the bent note with a slur to the non-bent note. When a dip is present on a bent note (3' B-flat), you will start below the pitch of the bent note (slightly below B-flat)—ending at the notated pitch (B-flat).	C1 p69 BB p18 BHTDVD12
Cut Small upside-down "V" above a note	 2" 1	The opposite of a Dip—note starts at the natural (unbent) pitch and quickly bends downward (around a half step). The articulations Dow, Gow or Cow work well.	BH2 p11
Staccato Dot above note head	 4	Note still receives its full note value, but is played short. (such as a "Ta," not holding the note after articulating).	General Notation
Shake Three slashes above or below note head(s)	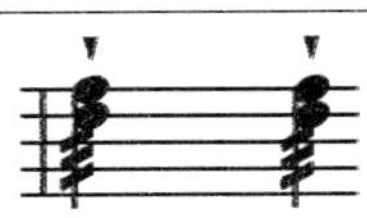 5 5 4 4	Shake between lower and upper notes. Rule of thumb is to start with the lower note and then start the shake to the upper note. Most draw shakes start with a dip. You can open your embouchure a bit to allow a little of the other note to bleed for a dirtier shake. You can also shake in an octave or fake-octave embouchure.	BB p17 C1 p42 BHTDVD12
Slap Small open circle above note head	 4 4 4	Same as standard tongue block (lips over four holes, tongue blocks three left holes), but the tongue starts off the harmonica, sounds the chord, and then slaps down to leave one note sounding (similar to saying "Hal"). This is considered a common tongue block technique and is not notated in my newer books and transcriptions.	BB p24 C2 p18 BHTDVD12 EX3, BBC
Flutter Tongue Same notation as shake, but notice there is no second note for a shake	 6+ 6+	Same embouchure as slap, but tongue travels on (single note) and off (chord) the harmonica to create a "flutter-like" effect.	C2 p26 BHTDVD12 EX3, BBC

Side-Flutter Tongue Small squiggly line between note heads	 6+ 3+	Same embouchure as flutter tongue, but tongue moves left to right. Typically the flutter is between octave notes; but you can use the tip of your tongue, covering fewer holes, for a larger chord sound.	Little Walter's "Off The Wall," 5th Chorus
Glissando Line ascending or descending to note head	 4 2	Slide between the two notes that are connected by the glissando. When there is no starting note for the glissando, slide from two or more notes above or below the target note, depending on the direction of the line.	C1 p38 BHTDVD12
Note Combination	 4 4 4 3 3 3	The addition of an upper note for a thicker texture (sometimes referred to as a double-stop). The volume of the upper note (how much air you allow to flow into the upper hole) depends on how strong a chord sound you want. If only a little bit of the upper note is added, I will use parentheses on the upper tablature hole number to show that only a little bit of air should leak into the upper hole.	General Music Notation
Quartertone Small plus (+) above a note head	 4' 4+ 3'	Half of a half step bend. Basically, it is a very slight bend. The example at left shows a half step bend for the tablature on the 3 draw (3' B-flat). The music notation shows the half step bend B-flat. The plus (+) above the note head indicates that the note should be played a quartertone higher than notated. For this instance you would play a pitch between the 3 draw and 3 draw half step bend. Quartertones are used often in blues—especially on the 3 draw in second position. If you do not bend enough, your line will sound very major (non-bluesy). If you bend the 3 draw too much, your line will sound very dark (more towards sounding minor than bluesy). You will see in the notation (and hear on recordings) that players will use many variations of the bend on the 3 draw. Listen carefully and do your best to match the player's pitch.	C2 p14 BHTDVD34
Grace Note Small note with slash on stem	 3' 2	A grace note indicates to play a note quickly before the next note. A grace note is used in place of a faster notated rhythm in the cases where the note is played so quickly that it does not make sense to place it in the normal stream of a line.	General Music Notation
Pull Slash-shaped note heads	 5+ 4 4 5+ 3 2 1	Tongue covers all four holes (no notes sound), slight pressure is built and tongue releases to sound chord. Unlike the Lift, the Pull is an articulation (more common).	BB p30 BHTDVD12 EX3, BBC, BH1
Octave Embouchure	 6+ 3+	An embouchure where four to five holes are covered by the lips and the tongue blocks the middle holes to sound the notes on the left and right, producing an octave. All common tongue block techniques can be used on the octave (slaps, pulls, side-pulls, pull-slaps, flutters, side-flutters, etc.).	BB p31 C2 p21 BHHTDVD12
Fake Octave	 2 6+ 5 2	Same as octave embouchure, but notes are not octaves (in our example at left the interval of a flat-7th is played).	BB p31 C2 p21 BHHTDVD12
Cough X-shaped note head with (C) in tablature	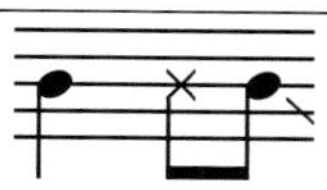 3 (C) 3	Similar to a Ghosted Note, but a strong cough is used to pronounce the note.	Magic Dick's "Whammer Jammer," 2nd Chorus
Wa	Wa	Note sounds with hands closed tightly, then hands open quickly creating a "Wa" sound.	BHTDVD12

Double Vibrato	Double Vibrato	Throat vibrato with slow hand tremolo.	William Clarke's "Lollipop Mama," 1st Chorus
Straight Eighths	Straight Eighths	A passage where the rhythm moves from a swing (triplet-based) feel to a straight (eighth note-based) feel.	William Clarke's "Blowin' the Family Jewels," 6th Chorus
Rhythmic Breathing & Ghosted Notes Thin, hollow-shaped note heads	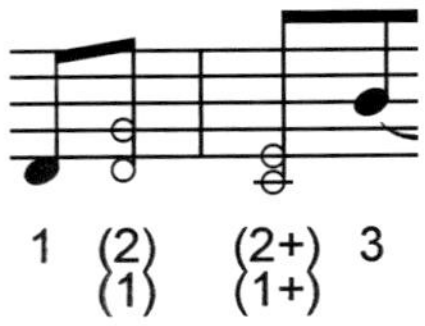	Rhythmic Breathing is used by players for rhythmic effect between main musical lines. These lines are not just breaths on the harmonica, but rhythmic elements that if not played present the song differently than the original. These should be played very softly. Ghosted Notes are basically the same, but are notes felt more than heard—note(s) may not sound, just the player's articulation is heard.	Magic Dick's "Whammer Jammer"

Chapter 14 – About the Author

David Barrett is the world's most prolific blues harmonica educator—leading the way in every facet of blues harmonica education for over twenty years.

The Early Years

Having played saxophone and trumpet as a youth, David already had a solid musical foundation before playing the harmonica at age fourteen. At age sixteen local harmonica legend Gary Smith took David under his wing as a private student. Gary also introduced David to the local blues scene and even invited him to participate is some of the local harmonica blowouts. By age eighteen David was studying music theory in college and started teaching harmonica at local music stores and institutes.

Author

By age twenty David had released his first book, Building Harmonica Technique, with one of the world's largest publishers, Mel Bay Publications. This book was the first serious blues harmonica method to be released in the market. David Barrett is now the world's most published author of blues harmonica lesson material, with over 60 book/CD sets and videos published.

David is also an active writer for various publications. He writes a featured column for Blues Revue Magazine called "Right On The Number" and is the editor and a writer for www.HarmonicaSessions.com® and the Harmonica Masterclass Workshop Free eZine.

Workshops

David is the founder and head instructor of Harmonica Masterclass Workshops. Founded in 1994, the focus of these workshops has been to make quality hands-on instruction available to the masses. Classes range in size from 20 participants to 250 participants, depending on program type and location. David also employs the top educators in the world for these workshops, such as Joe Filisko and Dennis Gruenling, as well as top artists in today's blues harmonica music scene.

David also teaches, judges and performs at other prestigious events, such as Hohner's World Harmonica Festival and Steve Baker's Harmonica Masters Workshop in Trossingen, Germany.

Private Lessons

Since age eighteen David has been teaching blues harmonica lessons full-time. In 2002 David founded School of the Blues in San Jose, California—the first school in the world for the specific study of blues music. David and his instructors (Guitar, Bass, Organ/Keyboard/Piano, Vocals, and Drums) teach private lessons and workshops as well as fly-in lessons. David teaches on average fifty private students a month. David is also active in working with local hospitals, teaching his Harmonica for Fun & Health classes to people with COPD (Emphysema), asthma and heart disease.

Performing and Recording Artist

David is a Grammy Nominated blues harmonica player for his work on John Lee Hooker Jr's album *All Odds Against Me*. He performs regularly in the California Bay Area (San Francisco Blues Festival, Monterey Bay Blues Festival, etc.) and abroad (Chicago, Germany, etc.). Recently he played as a featured artist in the Mark Hummel Blues Harmonica Blowouts, alongside James Cotton, Charlie Musselwhite, Kim Wilson, and Mark Hummel. David has recorded three albums, *Serious Fun*, *We Are The Blues* and the *History of the Blues Harmonica Concert*.

David has Worked or Played with:

Charlie Musselwhite, Mark Hummel, Lee Oskar, Rod Piazza, James Harman, James Cotton, Gary Smith, Andy Just, Mark Ford, Billy Boy Arnold, Jason Ricci, Rick Estrin, Paul deLay, Jerry Portnoy, Gary Primich, Howard Levy, Magic Dick, Tom Ball, Sonny Jr, John Mayall, Annie Raines, Paul Oscher, Phil Wiggins, Brendan Power, Sam Myers, Snooky Pryor, Steve Baker, Rob Paparozzi, Dennis Gruenling, Carlos del Junco, Mitch Kashmar, John Mayall, Joe Filisko, Lazy Lester, Kim Wilson, Kenny Neal, Peter "Madcat" Ruth, Junior Watson, Rusty Zinn, Nick Moss, Steve Freund, Johnny Cat, and John Garcia.

More Method Material by Author David Barrett

Harmonica Masterclass® Complete Blues Harmonica Lesson Series

Series 1 (Beginning)

1. Basic Blues Harmonica Method BK/CD (MB99103BCD)
2. Basic Blues Harmonica Method DVD (MB99104DVD)
3. Blues Harmonica Jam Tracks & Soloing Concepts #1 BK/CD (MB99105BCD)

Series 2 (Intermediate)

4. Classic Chicago Blues Harp #1 BK/CD (MB99106BCD)
5. Blues Harmonica Jam Tracks & Soloing Concepts #2 BK/CD (MB99110BCD)
6. Scales, Patterns, & Bending Exercises #1 BK/CD (MB99109BCD)
7. Exploring 2nd Position BK/CD (MB99183BCD)
8. Exploring 3rd Position BK/CD (MB99184BCD)
9. Building Harmonica Technique DVD #1 & #2 (MB99107DVD)

Series 3 (Advanced)

10. Classic Chicago Blues Harp #2 BK/CD (MB99111BCD)
11. Blues Harmonica Jam Tracks & Soloing Concepts #3 BK/CD (99115BCD)
12. Scales, Patterns, & Bending Exercises #2 B/2xCDs (99112BCD)
13. Exploring 1st Position BK/CD (MB99185)
14. Basic Blues Chromatic for the Diatonic Player BK/CD (MB99186BCD)
15. Building Harmonica Technique DVD #3 & #4 (MB99113DVD)

School of the Blues Lesson Series

David is the author of all the harmonica books and coauthor of all the books below for other instruments

16. Improvising Blues Harmonica BK/CD (MB20943BCD)
17. Blues Harmonica Accompaniment Playing (MB21385BCD)

Play-Along Trax

18. Blues Harmonica Play-Along Trax (MB21055BCD)
19. Blues Guitar Play-Along Trax (MB21059BCD)
20. Blues Keyboard Play-Along Trax (MB21062BCD)
21. Blues Bass Play-Along Trax (MB21064BCD)
22. Blues Drums Play-Along Trax (MB21067BCD)

Method Books – Level 1

23. Blues Harmonica, Level 1 (MB21053BCD)
24. Blues Guitar, Level 1 (MB21057BCD)
25. Blues Keyboard, Level 1 (MB21060BCD)
26. Blues Bass, Level 1 (MB21063BCD)
27. Blues Drums, Level 1 (21066BCD)

Method Books – Level 2

28. Blues Harmonica, Level 2 (MB21054BCD)
29. Blues Guitar, Level 2 (MB 21058BCD)
30. Blues Keyboard, Level 2 (MB 21061BCD)
31. Essential Blues Bass Lines (MB 21065BCD)

More Method Material

Here are some more method books and CDs from David Barrett

32. Building Harmonica Technique BK/CD (95167BCD)
33. Complete Classic Chicago Blues Harp BK/CD (MB95452BCD)
34. C Harmonica Blues Play-Along Tracks 2xCDs (MB20004CDB)
35. First Lessons Blues Harmonica BK/CD/DVD (MB20180SET)
36. First Lessons Harmonica BK/CD/DVD (MB20118BCD & DVD)
37. Blues Harp Licks Chart Bklt/CD (MB20719BCD)
38. Harmonica Position Chart (MB20720)
39. Harmonica Wall Chart (20291)
40. Youth Harmonica Method BK/CD (MB20092BCD)
41. Adult Harmonica Method BK/CD (MB20093BCD)
42. Harmonica for Fun & Health (MB20083)
43. Basic Harmonica Method BK/CD (MB96699BCD)
44. Gig Savers: Essential Harmonica Theory (MB20170)
45. Gig Savers: Essential Harmonica Scales (MB20171)
46. Gig Savers: Essential Harmonica Quick Charts (MB20172)
47. Gig Savers: Harmonica Microphones (MB20173)
48. Gig Savers: Harmonica Amplifiers (MB20174)
49. Gig Savers: First Harmonica Gig - Everything You Need to Know (MB20175)
50. Pocket Book Series: Blues Harp Classics Pocketbook (MB0786625015)
51. Pocket Book Series: Blues Harp Pocketbook (MB0786624558)
52. Fun with the Harmonica - CD & DVD Only (MB93305CD & MB 93305DVD)

Recordings

David Barrett is featured on the following recordings

1. *Serious Fun* – David Barrett & John Garcia (2003)
2. *We Are The Blues* – School of the Blues All-Star Band Live in the Studio (2005)
3. *History of the Blues Harmonica Concert* – With Joe Filisko, Dennis Gruenling, Kinya Pollard, Rusty Zinn, John Garcia and the School of the Blues All-Star Band (2010)

Thanks To:

1) Musicians:
   a) John Garcia (Guitar) – Thank you for all your help with the grooves and great ideas on "Butter Strut," your contribution to this book was huge!
   b) Frank De Rose (Bass) & Kevin Coggins (Drums) – Thank you both for your ideas on "Butter Strut"
2) Recording:
   a) Backing tracks for "Butter Strut" and "Whammer Jammer" recorded by Sam Curtis at THATRECORDCOMPANY in Morgan Hill, California (thatrecordcompany.com).
   b) All other recording done at School of the Blues in San Jose, California
3) Amplifiers:
   a) I record and perform with the MegaTone WEZO-45 Amplifier (megatoneamps.com). All amplified recording on the accompanying CD was done with this amplifier, minus "Whammer Jammer," which was recorded on a 1967 Fender Princeton Reverb
4) Harmonicas
   a) I play Hohner Marine Band Harmonicas (hohnerusa.com) customized by Joe Filisko (joefilisko.com)
5) Proof Reading:
   a) Diane Smith
   b) Dennis Carelli